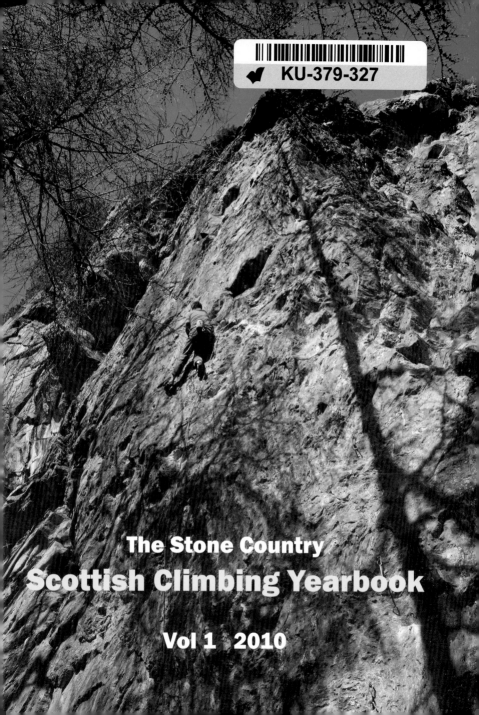

The Stone Country
Scottish Climbing Yearbook

Vol 1   2010

Edited by John Watson

Published by Stone Country Press 2010
61 Sinclair Drive, Glasgow, G42 9PU

www.stonecountry.co.uk

ISBN 978-0-9548779-5-8

Front Cover: Adrian Crofton on The Swirl, Raven Crag, Rhiconich

Back Cover: Kev Shields soloing The Benny Hill Show E3 The Quadrocks
Photo courtesy Steve Gordon

Verso Page: Ben Lomond in a winter inversion

☐ Nic Duboust onsight attempt of Marlena, Cave Crag 2009

Contents

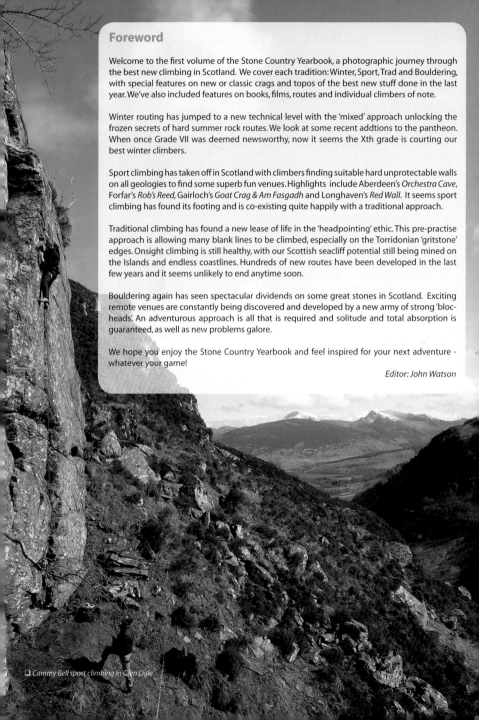

Foreword

Welcome to the first volume of the Stone Country Yearbook, a photographic journey through the best new climbing in Scotland. We cover each tradition: Winter, Sport, Trad and Bouldering, with special features on new or classic crags and topos of the best new stuff done in the last year. We've also included features on books, films, routes and individual climbers of note.

Winter routing has jumped to a new technical level with the 'mixed' approach unlocking the frozen secrets of hard summer rock routes. We look at some recent addtions to the pantheon. When once Grade VII was deemed newsworthy, now it seems the Xth grade is courting our best winter climbers.

Sport climbing has taken off in Scotland with climbers finding suitable hard unprotectable walls on all geologies to find some superb fun venues. Highlights include Aberdeen's *Orchestra Cave*, Forfar's *Rob's Reed*, Gairloch's *Goat Crag & Am Fasgadh* and Longhaven's *Red Wall*. It seems sport climbing has found its footing and is co-existing quite happily with a traditional approach.

Traditional climbing has found a new lease of life in the 'headpointing' ethic. This pre-practise approach is allowing many blank lines to be climbed, especially on the Torridonian 'gritstone' edges. Onsight climbing is still healthy, with our Scottish seacliff potential still being mined on the Islands and endless coastlines. Hundreds of new routes have been developed in the last few years and it seems unlikely to end anytime soon.

Bouldering again has seen spectacular dividends on some great stones in Scotland. Exciting remote venues are constantly being discovered and developed by a new army of strong 'bloc-heads'. An adventurous approach is all that is required and solitude and total absorption is guaranteed, as well as new problems galore.

We hope you enjoy the Stone Country Yearbook and feel inspired for your next adventure - whatever your game!

Editor: John Watson

❏ *Cammy Bell sport climbing in Glen Ogle*

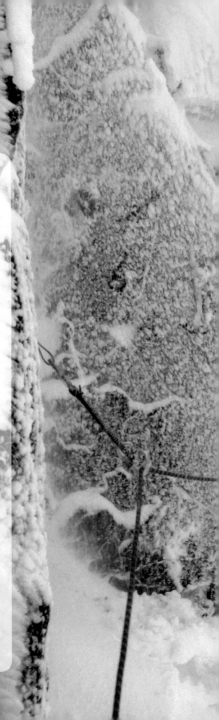

Winter

Scottish Winter 2008/09 - the epics!

Chop Suey VIII 8 > West Central Wall, Beinn Eighe
Guy Robertson & Tony Stone > 2008
'I used Tony's axe and head torch and nailed the pitch with steam comin' oot ma ears ...'

Hung Drawn and Quartered VIII 8 > Skye Am Basteir
Martin Moran & Nick Carter > Nov 2008

The God Delusion IX 9 > Beinn Bhan
Pete Benson & Guy Robertson > 10 Dec 2008
'The crux is akin to a highball 7a+ boulder problem, but on turf and with a leg-snapping penalty clause...'

Sassenach IX 9 > Carn Dearg, Ben Nevis
Andy Turner & Tony Stone > Dec 2008

Full Frontal VII,8 > Grey Corries
Viv Scott & Tony Stone > Dec 2008
'extreme ledge shuffling'

Devastation VII,8 > Ben Nevis
Ian Parnell & Andy Benson > Dec 2008

Brass Monkey VII 8 > Ben Nevis
Pete Davies & Tim Marsh > Dec 2008

Heidbanger > Ben Nevis
Rich Cross & Andy Benson > Dec 2008
'Thirty foot of teetering, thin hooks, long reaches, and spaced pro finally brought a blob of turf into reach...'

Metamorphosis VIII 9 > Ben Nevis
Iain Small & Gareth Hughes > Dec 2008

Yo Bro VIII 9 > Mullach nan Coirean, Mamores
Dave MacLeod > Dec 2008
'The climbing was harder than the final of the dry tooling comp the night before, but without the luxury of bolts...'

Bruised Violet VIII 8 > Beinn Eighe
Ian Parnell & Andy Turner > 10 March 2009
'A phenomenal direct line through the very steep ground Chop Suey avoids... at the top of the grade.'

❏ Jason Currie new routing on Lochnagar
Photo Adrian Crofton

Scottish Winter Action

Aside from the almighty Ben, winter new routes are being unzipped by supreme opportunists on the west coast hills such as Beinn Bhan and Beinn Eighe, once haunt of the legendary overnight raids from London by Mick Fowler. These fickle corries were the scene of two spectacular new mixed routes in December 2008 when Guy Robertson and Tony Stone took advantage of perfect brief conditions to climb *Chop Suey VIII 8* on Beinn Eighe's West Central Wall. Pete Benson and Guy Robertson finally succeeded on the almighty *God Delusion* on Beinn Bhan, an unforgiving direct IX 9 soaring through the superb line of *The Godfather*. *Chop Suey* saw a direct line cut through it in March 2009 by Ian Parnell and Andy Turner to give *Bruised Violet VIII 8*. Though Beinn Bhan (and Beinn Eighe) are massive and perfect for such new routing, their maritime position provides perfect conditions only occasionally and the timing is something of an art in itself.

Ben Nevis is becoming a popular early season venue for hardcore new-style mixed on very thin and steep rocky ground. With not as much turf as the NW venues, the new routes here are snowed up rock extremes, and with plenty of these unclimbed in winter, it looks like development will continue here into the Xth grades. Ethical purists may be spitting crampon teeth, but the big routes climbed here in the last year or so were in proven good snowy nick. *Sassenach IX 9* was climbed by Andy Turner and Tony Stone in December 2008, a typical sustained and technical 'new breed' ascent of a hard Ben rock route. Other notable routes on the Ben were *Devastation VII 8* by Ian Parnell and Andy Benson, as well as *Brass Monkey VII 8* by Pete Davies and Tim Marsh. Rich Cross and Andy Benson also added *Heidbanger VIII 8*, an impressive onsight ascent after repeating *Sioux Wall VIII 8*, (an earlier precursor to the Ben's new hardcore winter scene). Iain Small and Gareth Hughes also climbed *Metamorphosis* (a hard summer E2) to give a grand VIII 9.

Elsewhere, Dave MacLeod raided his now neighbourly Mamores to find *Yo Bro VIII 9* on Mullach nan Coirean and earlier in the season (Nov 2008) Martin Moran and Nick Carter ascended the north face of Am Basteir to give *Hung, Drawn and Quartered VIII 8*. Ian Parnell and Andy Turner repeated *The Duel IX 9* and Viv Scott and Tony Stone found the impressive *Full Frontal VII 8* in the Grey Corries.

Avalanches continue to pose a threat, with one terrible tragedy on the Buchaille in January 2009 claiming three lives. The new SAIS avalanche website is well worth checking out: *www.sais.gov.uk*

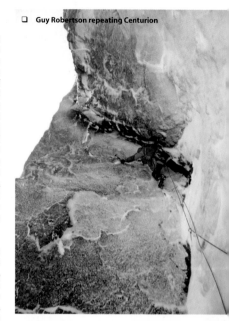
❑   **Guy Robertson repeating Centurion**

❑   **Tony Stone new routing on Beinn Eighe**

At the start of the second last pitch – 40m, 5b in summer – with 45 mins of daylight left, my axe got stuck in a crack. Then I dropped my head torch! So I used Tony's axe and head torch and nailed the pitch with steam comin' oot ma ears! Then, as Tony was seconding the pitch, after I had lowered down the only remaining head torch, Tony dropped it. It was pitch dark... somehow, we managed to bullshit our way up the final 5a pitch...

Guy Robertson on an epic ascent

It is a common practice for the Southern Highland ice climber to view the cliffs above Bridge of Orchy as the barometer of winter conditions. *Creag Coire and Dothaidh* is the frontal cliff above Bridge of Orchy and can easily be spied from the A82. If the ice has 'touched down' on *Fahrenheit 451*, things are good and nearby Udlaidh will certainly be in nick. If black, it's further north... However, even if half formed, many of the routes are still possible, if a grade harder due to lean mixed cruxes on the slabby walls and corners. *Salamander Gully* is the obvious icefall high on the left and is a reliable ice climb after a few days snow and freeze. Routes rely on turf as well as ice, so take a good mixed bag of gear - screws, warthogs, slings and drive-ins.

Approach: From the parking at the train station above the Bridge of Orchy hotel, go under the subway and onto the path that follows the burn directly up into *Coire an Dothaidh* (usually pronounced Corrie an Doughy). This leads up to the obvious bealach (col) descent between *Beinn an Dothaidh* and *Beinn Dorain*, which is the best descent. This approach only takes about an hour and is usually fast due to the corrie never holding much snow.

❑ **Salamander Gully**

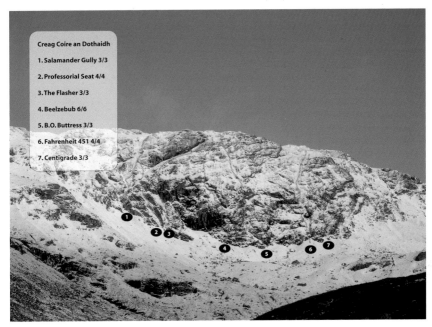

Creag Coire an Dothaidh
1. Salamander Gully 3/3
2. Professorial Seat 4/4
3. The Flasher 3/3
4. Beelzebub 6/6
5. B.O. Buttress 3/3
6. Fahrenheit 451 4/4
7. Centigrade 3/3

Creag Coire an Dothaidh

❏ **1. Salamander Gully** III/3
The obvious groove on the far left usually freezes into an attractive tumble of short icefalls. Climb in two or three enjoyable pitches to easy ground above the falls, with a rock belay below the falls on the left.

❏ **2. The Professorial Seat** IV/4
Just right of *Salamander* is a series of grooves and slabby corners leading eventually to join the icefalls. First belay in a snowy bay.

❏ **3. The Flasher** III/3
Slabby corner just right again trending left to a short corner, continue up to finish right along easy snow shelf under high cliffs.

❏ **4. Beelzebub** VI/6
An intricate line solving the icy slabs and blocking walls just left of the crest. Climb turf and icy grooves to belay below a red wall, then take the easiest line through the slabs and corners above to a snowfield. Further slabby climbing leads to a belay under a roof, then take the ice on the left to icy grooves trending right to top.

❏ **5. B.O.Buttress** III/3
Climb the central buttress on mixed ground on its right, belaying at the red wall, then follow further corners and short walls to the top.

❏ **6. Fahrenheit 451** IV/4
A superb long ice climb when in full raiment. Climb the obvious ice falls in several pitches, starting in the corner at the right of the corrie wall. The first pitches are the steepest and it continues scenically and eases at the top. Can be gained from the next route if lean.

❏ **7. Centigrade** III/3
The grooves and slabs to the right, belaying at a cave then breaking up and left to icy slabs and a step left onto the top of the icefall to finish. Short rocky corners can be taken to add technical interest.

Creag an Socach is the steep black cliff on the right on the walk in and its lines only become obvious on approach: the right hand corner ramp and icefall (if in nick) is the classic **Messiah VII 7** which needs a long freeze to be at its almighty best. **False Rumour Gully IV 4** is the excellent short gully on the far left, but also needs a long freeze to touch down.

Ben Nevis, Number 3 Gully Buttress

1

No. 3 Gully

5

3, 4

2

Number 3 Gully Buttress

1. Quickstep V
2. Knuckleduster VIII
3. Sioux Wall VIII
4. Thompson's Route IV
5. Gargoyle Wall VI

Right at the back of Coire na Ciste, a good hour's walk beyond the CIC hut, the snowy passage of Number Three Gully cuts through a very steep band of crags guarding the plateau. Number Three Gully Buttress describes the area of crag between Green Gully on the left through to Number Three Gully itself. The left hand side is slabby and ill-defined, but as the crag swings round to form the sidewall of the gully it rears up to an impressive 100m thrust of vertical and seemingly blank rock. The rock is well suited to modern mixed climbing techniques and, being high on the mountain, the routes come very readily into condition. The climbs rely almost exclusively on hooking and torqueing snowed-up rock, with only the occasional use of snow and dribbles of ice. The reliability of conditions on this part of the Ben was a major factor in the crag's development. It was during a poor ice season that Simon Richardson and Chris Cartwright started exploring the mixed climbing possibilities in 1996. They began on the other side of Number Three Gully with an ascent of the now classic *Cornucopia* (VII,8). In 2004 Bruce Poll and Tony Shepard were the first to make a winter ascent of the central bastion of Number Three Gully Buttress via the summer line of *Arthur* (HVS). Over the next few seasons most of the remaining summer lines fell, to produce a trio of hard grade VIII's.

Blair Fyffe

No. 3 Gully Buttress Classic Winter Routes

❑ **Gargoyle Wall VI 6   Carrington & Nicolson 1977**
Climbed in the dying days of 1977, this demanding mixed route was well ahead of its time - an indicator of trends that would occur twenty years later. Named after a projecting block high up clearly visible from the gully, the route takes a devious line through some steep ground on the right flank of the central bastion. It is now a popular classic, and a fine introduction to the harder mixed routes, but be warned, it can become verglassed and bold, and in these conditions has been known to stop strong climbers in their tracks.

❑ **Sioux Wall VIII 8   Parnell & Metheral 2006**
This imposing line blasts straight up a line of shallow grooves in the right centre of the compact buttress. Good cracks and positive edges make it much more amenable than it's fearsome appearance suggests. Spectacular positions and sustained but never desperate climbing mean this route has become the most climbed grade VIII on the mountain, and arguably in Scotland.

❑ **Knuckleduster VIII 9   Fyffe & Ashworth 2007**
A truly awe-inspiring line, plundering the striking groove in the heart of the steepest section of crag, and visible from the C.I.C hut. The intimidation factor is amplified in the knowledge that an early attempt ended in the local hospital with numerous broken bones! The short second pitch, traversing out of the main groove up a steep wall is probably the crux. However, the long, sustained and not overly well protected third pitch should not be underestimated.

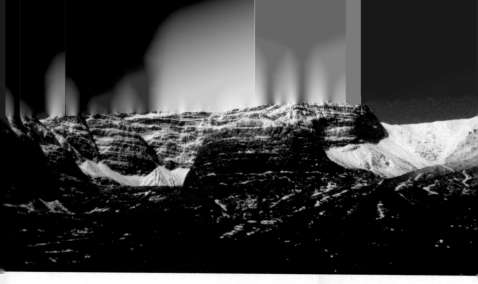

❏ **The God Delusion** 240m IX,9
Beinn Bhan, G Robertson & P Benson 10 December 2008

'An outstanding, complex and aggressive voyage up the heart of the mighty Godfather wall. The climbing is sustained all the way, and in places bold and strenuous.' Pete Benson.

The lower wall is based on the left hand of the two right-trending weaknesses. Start about 20m metres left of *The Godfather*, at a prominent chimney slot. **1.** Climb the slot, then go left for a few metres before climbing back up right to a ledge and belay by a short groove and rib (20m). **2.** Step right to gain and follow the awkward slim ramps trending right pas a wide crack and hard mantelshelf. Continue up the easier fault to gain the snow bay then move up and left to belay left of the corner (30m) **3.** Climb the short wall on the left, then traverse hard right below an overhanging fault to a difficult step down across the top of the corner (20m) **4.** Steep cracks up the left-hand diagonal weakness are followed with sustained interest to the balcony, then continue direct to belay below huge overhangs (40m). **5.** Traverse left to join Godfather pitch 3 at the short fierce groove, but above this go hard right to belay below a prominent crack above the overhangs overhead (30m) **6.** Go up to below the first groove left of the crack. Pull over the overhang into the groove and follow it to a ledge. Work up first right then back left to another ledge below a more substantial overhanging section. Above is a smooth corner groove. Right of this, and using a good thin crack to get started, pull desperately up right into a turfy niche. Swing out right onto the edge, then climb steeply up moving back slightly leftwards to a good ledge (40m). **7.** Mantle up into the corner above, then go hard left under a nose into a turfy fault which is followed to the upper terrace. Go left along this to an enormous block and cave belay below a wide crack (30m) **8.** Climb the blocky overhanging corner fault on the left to easier ground and the top (30m).

❏ The God Delusion > Beinn Bhan
Photo Guy Robertson

❑ **Night climbing on The God Delusion**
Photo courtesy Pete Benson

Sport

Ian Tayler on Mactalla 7a > Goat Crag

Sport Climbing in Scotland

Conglomerate Crags have become a fashionable geological addition to Scotland's growing sport crags. Notoriously hard to onsight, the rock pebbles produce pumpy blind climbing, like swimming through a bag of Minstrels. The best crags developed recently have been *The Camel*, above Loch Duntelchaig at Inverness, *Moy Rock* near Dingwall, *Kirriemuir* and *Rob's Reed* near Forfar, as well as *The Mound* and *Silver Rock* near Golspie. In July 2009, at *The Camel*, Andrew Wilby completed his project to give the Inverness scene another classic 8a in *Death Is A Gift*, taking the leaning wall up left of Dave Redpath's classic *Ubuntu 8a*.

The Camel

In the North West, Am Fasgadh, Goat Crag and Creag nan Luch were further developed by Paul Tatersall, Ian Taylor and Lawrence Hughes amongst others. Before he emigrated, Lawrence Hughes climbed the superb *Really Good Fun* F7c+ on the clean and impressive leaning prow of Goat Crag. Goat Crag and Am Fasgadh now provide the hardest and best sport climbing in the North West and are proving popular winter sports venues. Topos can be found at *www.wildwesttopos. com* with updates in 2010.

Goat Crag > Pic Ian Taylor

Dumbuck saw a number of new bolts added this year by Dave Redpath, John Watson and Stewart Brown, mainly due to corrosional issues, but also to reposition and extend certain lines (eg. *Awaken* now has proper protection and *Flesh for Fantasy* has additional bolts). Significant repeats were *Voodoo Magic 8b* by Redpath & Stewart Brown, *Happiness in Slavery* by Redpath, *So Be It 8a+* by Stewart Brown and Ben Litster, with the 7c's seeing many repeats.

Dunglass, a notoriously loose trad crag at Strathblane, north of Glasgow, was the scene of some resurrection in spring 2009 from John Watson & Colin Lambton. The original, sparsely bolted sports wall was grid bolted to provide a wider and safer mix of enjoyable mid-grade routes from 6a to 7b. Ardvorlich Crags were bolted further in 2009 and the superb Quarterdome crag is sprouting hard new routes. Topos will be available from *www.stonecountry.co.uk* in 2010.

Am Fasgadh > Pic Ian Taylor

Dunkeld is always busy in spring as trad-heads build stamina on Cave Crag. It's also the proving ground for strong onsight attempts, with Stewart Brown flashing *Hamish Ted's* on his first acquaintance with the crag. Nic Duboust came close to an onsight of *Marlena*, but bagged it second go. Cave Crag was to see a nefarious and anonymous debolting raid in June 2009, but the climbing community responded immediately with rebolting and restoration.

Dunglass Sports Wall

Orchestra Cave by Tim Rankin

Ambience:	'out there' sea-cave sport
Season:	all year, birds in summer
Gear:	70m ropes, jumars, biceps!
Rock:	unusual blobby schist
Grades:	7a to 8a+
OS GetaMap:	NO 944 979

Access as for Earnsheugh & Boglesheugh cliffs. From the A90, take the exit signed to Findon just north of Portlethen. After a few bends take the second left marked Findon Road. Drive through the village to the last house at the NW end. Park at the dirt track or in the village. Take a left down the track then veer right along the heathery moor by a stone wall. After 50m go straight across the fields to another stone wall to reach an inlet with a grassy south wall. Boglesheugh is the cliff south of this and the Orchestra Cave is hidden round on the seaward face just south again. It is best to abseil from a big block slightly south of the top anchor bolts and leave a rope in place for easier escape. 70m ropes essential.

❏   **Bassoon** ☽   25m 7a+
The left hand line of resin bolts up technical groove then through huge roof.

❏   **Double Bassoon**   35m 7c
As the name suggests the extension to the top of the cliff a big pitch! Tim Rankin 2009.

❏   **Air on a G string**   12m 7c/7c+
The line just left of *Dangleberries* to a lower off in the roof. There is a closed project extension above! Superb moves. Tim Rankin 2009.

❏   **Dangleberries** ☽   30m 8a+
Takes the central line through the full height of the cave. After a tricky 1st roof tackle the 45 degree wall, then pull through another large roof to a no-hands rest (double knee bar). Follow the vague groove above and pull through the final roof rightwards (crux) to the lower off. Brilliant pumpy climbing leading to a bouldery crux. Bailing out at the double bolt lower off at 20m provides an excellent 7c+. Ally Coull 2009.

❏   **Blobstrop** 👽   20m 8a
The steep line immediately right of *Dangleberries* has been described as a very worthy and classic 8a with great moves. Ally Coull 2009.

❏   The 'O Cave' > Bassoon 7a+ > Photo Neil Morrison

In the North East, Ally Coull and Tim Rankin abseiled into the big cave just south of Boglesheugh (left) and bolted a number of futuristic-looking lines. The 'Orchestra Cave', sport venue provided 30m of upside-down climbing amongst clamouring seabirds and crashing surf. In late 2008 Ally Coull succeeded on his mega-route *Dangleberries* to give Aberdeen a stunning 8a+ up a sequence of bizarre protuberances through the full height of the cave. Tim Rankin described the 'O Cave' as 'the best sport development I know of in Scotland over the last year', and we don't think he's wrong! The whole adventure of getting into the cave and the commitment involved in climbing such steep routes only adds to its already legend sports status.

Tim Rankin and friends also added bolted routes to the Red Quarry Wall in Longhaven. The walls of the quarry provided steep sports routes on two different walls. The highlight of 2009 was Gordon Lennox's ascent of *Dracula 8b* in October on woefully thin flakes. Along with Tim's desperate test *Lucifer 8b*, these are the hardest sports routes in the Aberdeen area at present and a popular proving ground for young redpointers (see the feature page on Red Wall Quarry).

❑ **The 'O Cave' > Ally Coull on Dangleberries 8a+ > Pic Pete Benson**

Red Wall Quarry by Tim Rankin

Ambience: hardcore quarrymen
Rock: red granite
Season: all year
Gear: steel fingers, 50m rope
Grades: F7a+ to F8b
GetaMap: NK 115 388

This large open quarry is probably the most easil
accessible of all the major Longhaven Quarrie
It is better known as a convenient access poir
to the Red Wall itself, one of the most impressiv
traditional climbing areas on the coast north c
Aberdeen. So far two different walls have bee
bolted: the obvious overhanging back wall of th
quarry below the descent and the not-so-obviou
steep slab on the south side of the quarry.

The rock is generally excellent granite if still
little crumbly under foot in places but this shoul
improve with traffic. Being granite and never tha
steep the climbing tends to be technical an
sustained with the overall quality of the climbin
being quite remarkable for quarried rock. Bot
walls face east and catch only the morning su
which can be an advantage in summer. The bac
wall does suffer from a persistent seep but only th
start of *The King* is affected and this can usually b
diverted to allow the holds to dry.

The most favourable conditions are found in th
morning on clear sunny or breezy days but a goo
work out can be had even in the worst damp day
as the climbing tends to be on positive holds. It i
also possible to climb on the back wall in light rai
or showers. All routes Tim Rankin 2008 /09 (excep
Dracula 2010 Gordon Lennox).

Approach
From Aberdeen take the A90 to Peterhead. Tur
right off the A90 onto a track just after Longhave
village 8 miles before Peterhead. Follow the track t
its end to a car park beside an old cottage. Follow
path past the cottage east then south in to the firs
Quarry works. Go right to the fence and pick u
another path which leads east on to the headlan
of the Red Wall. Continue on this path until it turn
south along the rim of the Red Quarry. Half wa
along the back of the quarry a steep grass ram
leads down to the floor of the quarry. The Back Wa
is obvious on the left of the descent facing out t
sea.   For the Bridal Slab approach from the Bac
Wall down a boulder field staying close to th
south edge of the quarry.

Back Wall

The most impressive wall in the quarry looks blank on first appearance and overhangs about 10 degrees. It gains height from left to right, the first route starts from the raised platform at the left end of the wall.

❏ **Jester**   10m 7b

The left hand line climbing cracks and flakes gives a reasonable warm up after the initial crux past the first 2 bolts. Bolted to allow for these moves to be pulled past to warm up but care must be taken clipping the 3rd bolt.

❏ **Messiah**   12m 7c+❂

The next thin crack to the right with resin bolts gives an excellent sustained struggle. Start as for *The King* and swing left into the crack. It seeps from the bottom of the initial crack but this doesn't affect the holds.

❏ **The King**   18m 7c+ ❂

The compelling central line weaving its way up flakes and edges. The start up the flake is unfortunately often wet but a rag in the top of the flake stems the flow and it quickly becomes dry to climb. Easy to do the moves but frustrating to red point. In the opinion of some it is low in the grade!

❏ **Dracula**   22m 8b ❂

The desperate thin flake leads to an even more desperate move to gain the good thin flake. A wander up this leads to the sustained upper wall and groove of the next route. The direct finish is a closed project. Gordon Lennox Oct 09

❏ **Lucifer**   20m 8b ❂

The skilfully enhanced blank wall leads to a semi rest at the undercut break then continues up the fine sustained upper wall and groove. The crux is a very height-dependent move above the rest and the route might well only be 8a+ for the average man!

❏ **Sultan**   12m 7c ❂

The blank looking wall just left of the right bounding corner gives a superb sustained face climb.

Bridal Slab

The huge inverted triangular slab is found at a lower level and to the south of the back wall routes. It has one route ❏ *Kingdom of Granite* 7a+ 22m.

❑ Mike Lee working the power moves of Spitfire at the Anvil

The Anvil

Ambience: hardcore blacksmiths
Rock: good schist and quartz
Season: dry spell spring & autumn
Gear: Gri-Gri, energy bars, 50m rope
Grades: F6b to 8c+
GetaMap: NS206949

'The Anvil' is the biggest boulder in Scotland! It hides in remote conifer woods and is only visible from Carrick Castle across Loch Goil. It is one hour easy walk from Lochgoilhead, quicker with bikes. Park in the village and walk along the residential road along the shore for a mile to a path leading up through the forest onto the main forestry road. Follow this south for what seems ages, round a dipping bend and burn and up again. As the road descends after 2km to a flatter section, and directly opposite Carrick Castle, look out for an orange marker on the left. The giant block lies 20m uphill.

Sport Routes R-L

❑ **Way Out West** F6c
The right arête to ledge, then rock hard left to surmount final bulge.

❑ **Nu Mettle** F7b
Shallow right-trending groove to join *Way Out West*. Sloping holds.

❑ **Hammertime** ☾ F7b+
Main diagonal right on edges and pockets from first bolt of *Black Out*.

❑ **Black Out** F8b
Malcolm Smith's testpiece straight up from *Hammertime*.

❑ **Crossfire** F7c+
Diagonal up *Hammertime* left through *Spitfire*, left along to *Anvilfire* LO.

❑ **Spitfire** ☾ F8a+
The red wall is fingery then dynamic with big moves to top quartz.

❑ **Anvilfire** F7c+
The left arête of the front face onto the hanging slab at top.

❑ **Friendly Fire** ☾ F7a
Up *Anvilfire* to first bolt, then left to slab and final juggy groove.

❑ **Atlantic Strikes Back** F7c+
The steep groove onto ledge and ramp above right to *Friendly Fire* LO.

❑ **Cowal Crusaders** F6c
Alt. start to *Friendly Fire*. Ramp on the left and gain the ledge of original.

❑ **The Smiddy** ♥ F8b+
The wall right of *Shadowlands*. At crack crux right to a jump finish.

❑ **Shadowlands** ☾ F7c
Classic cave arête via the long crack. Cave start to ledge then crack.

❑ **Fire Power** F8b
Right side of the Anvil roof, starting right of the short arête.

❑ **Blood Fire** F8a+
Up the corner to a line of flat holds into *Heavy Metal*.

❑ **Heavy Metal** F7b
Gain *Fire Power* at mid-height by step off the opposite boulder. Pre-clip!

❑ **Body Blow** F8b+
Top half of the roof. Step off boulder and power up the headwall!

❑ **Metalcore** ☾ F8c+
Body Swerve start to follow the right-trending crack all the way to the apex of roof.

❑ **Body Swerve** ♥ 8c
Far left-hand roof. Bouldery, fingery desperation to easier groove of *Amateur Hacker*.

❑ **Amateur Hacker** 6c
Climb round the prop boulder onto a shelf to slanting groove above.

❏ Busy day on the North Berwick slabs

North Berwick Law Sport

Ambience: east coast suntrap
Rock: fine ochre sandstone
Season: all year
Gear: 10 draws, wall rope
Grades: 5+ to 7c elim.
GetaMap: NT 555 839

North Berwick Law is one of Edinburgh's best climbing venues, catching all the sun going and usually bone dry. The small sandstone open-book quarry was developed by Rab Anderson and Bruce Kerr in 1989 but recent new routes have been added and much fun can be had with eliminates or linking routes, which are no more than 15m long.

Access: from the A1 east of Edinburgh, take the A1 to Haddington, exit onto the A6137 for North Berwick (10km), or catch the train from Edinburgh! Once in the town at the church, go uphill passing the school on the right into open country. Take the sudden side-road on a bend to parking under the domed hill of North Berwick Law. Follow the path right in two minutes to the quarry.

❑ 1. **Necktie**   F6b+
The left arête. Gain ledge then step right.
❑ 2. **Fogtown** ◐   F7a
Left hand wall with long reaches! (7a+ up Gravity).
❑ 3. **Eliminate Law**   F7c
The wall between *Fogtown* and *Law of Gravity*.
❑ 4. **Law of Gravity** ◐   F7a+
Crimp crux to ledge direct to top via long hauls.
❑ 5. **Jaws of the Law**   F6c
The first of 3 stretchy routes.
❑ 6. **Law of the Flies** ◉   F7a
A jump is usually required.
❑ 7. **Law and Disorder**   F6a+
The last route on the wall via niche and corner.
❑ 8. **Law of the Rings**   F7a
A left to right girdle about mid height.
❑ 9. **Darkness Falling** ◐   F6a+
Contortions in corner onto slab.
❑ 10. **The Brazilian**   F7a
Direct eliminate right of 9.
❑ 11. **Igneous Intruder**   F6c
The central slab.
❑ 12. **Old Law Breaker** ◐   F6b
Right hand slab route.
❑ 13. **Dosage**   F7a+
Direct of 12. via mono, trend left to tackle overlap.
❑ 14. **Wild Iris**   F5+
Right arête of the slab.
❑ 15. **Solitary Soul**   F6b
Far right of main quarry, by graffiti 'GBH'. 6m 2 bolts.
❑ 16. **Anarchic Law**   F6b
Arête to the right of 13 has 3 bolts and is 8m.

Dunglass Sport

Ambience: evening suntrap
Rock: blocky basalt
Season: all year
Gear: 10 draws, wall rope
Grades: 5 to 7b
GetaMap: NS 574 789

Dunglass is the domed basalt plug 1km east of Strathblane in North Glasgow, with its west wall providing good short power routes in the lower to mid grades. Approach: From Strathblane church car park on the Lennoxtown road, just east of the wee roundabout. Take the Lennoxtown path along the old disused railway until the crag comes into view in 10 minutes. Don't cross the fields early, but continue to a gate in front of the black face and walk west round the rock to the sports crag. Do not park at the farm please.

❑ 1. **Imodium Wall** ☯ F7a
Take the leaning green wall above pillar direct to slopey ledge step left to apex of steepness. Don't chicken out early, it's a good finish!

❑ 2. **Imodium Crack** F6a
The big left trending fault is gained from the top of the ramped pillar. Trend up right to horizontal niche, then left. Direct finish is 6a+.

❑ 3. **Whiplash** F6b
From the pillar step right to climb to a wee triangular cave, then take the black headwall. A clever hidden undercut makes this doable!

❑ 4. **Mister Poops** F6b+
The wall and high bulge just right of the base of the pillar, step off horizontal shelf via hard sequence to jugs. Turn roof on left. The 'spike' is a red herring...

❑ 5. **Poop Deck** F6c+
The shattered wall above shelf to gain top of *Bahama Breeze* crack. Exciting finish on hidden holds! Watch out for snappy holds.

❑ 6. **Bahama Breeze** F6c+
The ferned crack on juggy holds up left to a cracked bulge crux, surmount this with a difficult crossover sequence and finish confidently.

❑ 7. **Negotiations with Isaac** F6b
Step off shelf on right through embedded boulder bolt. Up the crack to giant rsting jugs then take the wall above. direct to Seam lower off.

❑ 8. **The Tanning Salon** F7b
Just right of shelf. Straight up past crack to bouldery crux to better holds, direct up wall to *Seam* LO.

❑ 9. **The Beef Monster** ☯ F6c+
Probably the best route here and the original! Step off right pedestal, up orange streaked bulge, right to layaways to niche then headwall to RH LO.

❑ 10. **The Seam** ☯ F7a+
Right of *Beef Monster* and climb the seam crack all the way past the old peg to finish direct up left to high LO. Pumpy and reachy last move!

❑ 11. **Airhead** F7a
The right hand bolt-line through the low bulging wall (crux) finish direct via a crimpy wall to final lower off. Another classic from Andy Gallagher.

❑ 12. **The Ring Cycle** ☯ F7b
Start up *The Seam* crux and cross through *Beef Monster* to reach the jugs on *Isaac* at half height. Climb left under the bulge and through top wall of *Whiplash* to the far left lower off.

❏ Cameron Bell getting obligatory tan on Airhead 7a at Dunglass

Ardvorlich Sport

Ambience: sunny walls
Rock: quartzy schist
Season: spring and autumn
Gear: 10 draws, wall rope
Grades: 6a to 7a
GetaMap: NN 322 122

These are the pleasant schist 'hidden walls' above Ardvorlich B&B on the west bank of Loch Lomond, 2km north of Inveruglas or 4km south of Ardlui.

They provide sunny pocketed wall climbing with grand views down Loch Lomond. Routes are no more than 18m, take slings to extend lower offs over the crag lip. Walk-off is easy from the top.

Make sure you go in spring or autumn on a sunny dry day - in summer the bracken is impenetrable. The higher crag 'Quarterdome' is the large open-book crag 15 minutes steep walk above the Hidden Walls and is currently in development.

Park discreetly by the barn at the entrance drive to Ardvorlich B&B, closing the gate behind you. Walk into the woods at the left side of the barn and turn right over a fence just before the railway track.

Walk under the railway culvert and scramble across the burn to a path on the right bank which leads up in five minutes to the Hidden Walls which appear suddenly, facing the mountainside.

❑ **1. Arm Carnage**   F7a
Boulder along the roofed crag at the left and lunge up to a ledge by the first bolt, follow this up and right to step across to join *That Sinking Feeling*. Often wet.

❑ **2. That Sinking Feeling**   F6a+
Tricky left arête to first bolt (pre-clip), then easier up to a scooped groove crux. Step through and finish left.

❑ **3. The Groove** 🌑   F6a
The central groove has good juggy climbing to a crux step up to pockets and an enjoyable final headwall. The holds are there! Mantel the top to lower off.

❑ **4. Drifting Too Far from Shore**   F6c
The bulge right of the groove, taken on the right via cunning. Headwall finish direct.

❑ **5. Lake Lomond** 🌑   F6a
After the initial cracked groove under the sapling, breathe deep and step left onto the superb headwall.

❑ **6. Dilemma**   F6a+
Right wall. Crux quartz pull through bulge and travel up right through 7 to finish direct to ledges at top.

❑ **7. Snake Eyes**   F6a
Pull through the central roof and go left to join with 6, step left and finish up juggy left ramp up to sapling, right to LO.

❑ **8. Magic Carpet Ride** 🌑   F6b
Bolts and pegs on thsi one, hold your nerve. The direct central line aiming for the very apex of the right wall.

Jo George on the excellent 'Lake Lomond' at Ardvorlich

Cave Crag Sport

Ambience: continental 'limestone'
Rock: chalky schist and quartz
Season: spring & autumn
Gear: 10 draws, 50m rope, clip-stick
Grades: 7b to 8a
GetaMap: NO 018438

From the A9 north of Perth turn off to Dunkeld, through village and turn right towards Blairgowrie A923. Take the second forestry track on left, this leads in 500m to the main forest car-park. Take the main pine-needled track left contouring the hill, it splits after 100m, fork right uphill to Lady Charlotte's cave. Uphill again behind this to steep path to crag.

❏   **Marlena** ☙   F7c
The classic left hand line of bolts past pockets and flakes to a right traverse at half height to the base of a diagonal left crack. Crux moves through this allow a final pumped stretch over a bulge for the jugs under the chain. D.Cuthbertson (1986)

❏   **Ultima Necat**   F7c
Start up *Marlena*, climb more directly and boldly from the 4th bolt direct up to lower off on left side of wall. Superb if a little run out! Mark McGowan (1987)

❏   **Hamish Ted's**   F7b+
Hamish Teddy's Excellent Adventure. Climb *Marlena* to the jugs at base of the crack, then step right to climb the juggier arête. D.McCallum (1992).

❏   **Silk Purse** ☙   F7c+
The line of bolts on the right has a crux groove section to rejoin *Marlena* at half-height, follow this via the crack to step right into the high right groove leading to a tenuous layback finish. G. Livingston (1987) An eliminate line between *Marlena* and *Silk Purse* is contrived but worth it for the 8a tick...

❏   **Silk Teddies**   F7c
Starting up *Silk Purse* into *Hamish Ted's* at *Marlena* junction is a popular combo route.

Marlena F7c - 10 step beta

1. Gaston presses to quartz holds
2. quartz sequence through the slot left to good edges
3. up to undercut block
4. up to flake or direct through pocket and crimp to jugs
5. handrail across and egyptian up to jugs under crack
6. shake out before crux crossover in crack
7. up to LH pinch sidepull
8. high step up to RH gaston and LH pocket
9. crank up high to RH slot
10. up to 2-finger slot, step high, cross to chain... success?

Dumbuck Sport

Ambience: volcanic eruption
Rock: basalt
Season: ouside of summer
Gear: 10 draws, wall rope, clip-stick
Grades: 6b to 8c
GetaMap: NO 018438

Regular trains from Glasgow Central underground to Dumbarton East run half-hourly. Turn left out of the station and walk along the main road to the Dumbuck Hotel (15 minutes). Take the Right of Way path round the hotel to the cycleway, cross the busy A82 carefully, walk along road right for 200m and enter the steep woods by an electricity box. A blue cord may be in situ to lead the way steeply up to the crag. Haul up the wee corner onto the belay ledges. If travelling by car, park at the hotel just opposite the Right of Way track (on left of hotel as you enter).

❑ **Ben Litster** on *So Be It* **8a+ Dumbuck**

Dumbuck Routes Left to Right

☐   **Dave Redpath repeating Voodoo Magic**

Rob's Reed

Ambience: 'outdoor climbing wall'
Rock: sandstone flag and conglomerate
Season: all year, except 1 Sep-31 Oct
Gear: 10 draws, wall rope
Grades: 5 to 7c
GetaMap: NO 488 523

A superb sandstone and conglomerate sports venue, this enjoyable crag has around 50 routes from the easy grades through to hard 7c roofs. Despite being no more than 20m high, it has a technical and pumpy 'onsight' feel, giving a testing day out whatever your level. Ticking the crag in one day is the big challenge!

The crag was developed by Scott Muir, Neil Shepherd, Ken Edwards, Derek Armstrong and Iain MacDonald from 2005 onward. It is perfect in spring and summer, catching pleasant shade in the hottest of summers, as well as being a reliable winter sports venue.

There is a climbing ban from Sep 1st to Oct 31st every year when deer are kept here, please note this!

For a full topo, access and news, please visit:
www.arbroathclimbing.webs.com

❑ John Watson on *Climb & Punishment* **7b**

Situated on the brow of Pitscandly Hill 2 miles east of Forfar, it is easy to reach from the A90. Drive through Forfar and take the B9113 exit to Montrose. After 2 miles you pass a quarry and some small cottages, before a missable sign for Wemyss Farm. Drive dead slow up here to a sharp left turn then a hairpin bend. Park OFF the road and walk along the track for 30m, hop the deerfence on the right and climb the grass slope. The path descends left in 300m to the crag. Divided into several 'sectors' split by obvious features, from right to left on approach:

1. Main Wall - Routes 1-13
2. Elder's Wall - Routes 14-23
3. Size Isn't Everything Sector - Routes 24-30
4. Sector Caravan - Roof Routes 31-37
5. Dirty Harry's Cave - Big roof routes 38-46

❑   **Going Through on Aggregate** ⚲ F7a
The first orange wall on approach has a direct line on pink hangers through the capping roof at the top. Technical low-down, butch high up.

❑   **Autobahn** ⚲   F6c+
Elder's Wall. The first prominent crack in good sandstone flag is followed to a twinned conglomerate crack finish.

❑   **Grand Theft Auto** ⚲   F7a
Elder's Wall. Another fine crack climb just left again. Crux sequence gains the wee roof to take the finger crack above.

❑   **Trailer Trash** ⚲   F7b+
Sector Caravan. The first low giant roof is climbed powerfully to an easier groove section above. Bouldery and bizarre.

❑   **Dirty Harry** ⚲   F6b
Dirty Harry's Cave. Climbs the right side of the cave via a groove, then breaks left onto headwall to finish.

❑   **The Enforcer** ⚲   F7b+
Dirty Harry's Cave. Climbs the central right roof through two roofs to a crux wall before the final small roof.

❑   **Climb and Punishment** ⚲ F7b
Dirty Harry's Cave. Climbs the left side of the cave via two roofs to a headwall finish. Awesome!

❑ **Colin Lambton** *Going Through on Aggregate* **7a at Rob's Reed**

Trad

Scottish Trad Updates

Traditional rock climbing in the last few years has been accused of disappearing without trace in Scotland as the younger generation take to sport and bouldering to challenge their high physical standards. This is not necessarily the case, however - the new fashion for 'headpointing' is opening up hard short crag routes in traditional areas that were unjustifiable before and perfect for the gym-honed generation who can warm up on E5's. Foremost on this front have been climbers like Gordon Lennox, Guy Robertson, Tim Rankin, Dave MacLeod, Ben Litster, Nic Duboust, Graham Tyldsley, Niall McNair and Kev Shields, to name but a few.

❏ Neil Morrison on Saruman E4 > Longhaven
Photo Neil Morrison collection

Dave MacLeod continued his assaults on the toughest geology Scotland can provide. He visited the 'Red Gritstone' of Torridon in the summer of 2009 and succeeded on two new E8's and an E9: *Kelvinator E8 6c* and *Kolus E8 6c*. Both routes are located on the immaculate terraced buttresses on Seana Mheallan. Dave returned to straighten out *Kelvinator* to give the more direct *Present Tense E9 7a*. Of *Kelvinator* he notes the 'gritstone' flavour of Torridon:

'One line was to bear-hug up the fridge block and do a weird rotation palming move into the niche on the left - sort of like the move at the top of the groove on Gaia, but a fair bit harder'

❏ Jonathan Lagoe on Black Gold Pitch 2, Barra
Photo Colin Moody

Dave took a bigger imagination to Orkney's Hoy cliffs during the summer and autumn, attempting a huge multi-pitch big wall route with F8c pitches on the Longhope Route on Hoy, home to Britain's longest vertical climb. Things at these latitudes do not go smoothly. Dave wrote of his frustrations:

'I made the journey back to Hoy, over Cuilags and across the plateau once again and uncoiled my ropes in mist and the ever present buffeting gale at the edge of the cliff. I threw a coil of rope into the mist, but it blew right back over me. I watched the fulmars for a bit while I got ready to do a 'bag rap' to get over the edge in the wind. But the arrival of rain on the raging wind soaked everything within seconds and there was nothing for it but to jog back over the plateau like a drowned rat...'

This epic route did not see an ascent this year due to the near-impossible logistics but it's certain to fall at some point and will be a challenger to Dave's own *Echo Wall* as Scotland's hardest trad route. Echo Wall itself still remains ungraded and unrepeated after its beautifully filmed first ascent (which rightly won Claire MacLeod a BAFTA award). The unspoken thought remains that we might just have an E12 in Scotland.

❏ Dave MacLeod on Present Tense E9 > Seana Mheallan
Photo Claire MacLeod www.davemacleod.com

Southern Highlands

Dumbarton has little room left for new routes, but repeats of hard classics abound. Ben Litster succeeded on another repeat of *Requiem* E8 in the summer of 2009 (placing all the gear on lead after practise) and to the left Nic Duboust quietly onsighted *Chemin de Fer* E5, both repeats a healthy sign of a strong generation coming through. Cambusbarron Quarry saw a popular resurgence on the cracklines and walls, with Niall McNair reclimbing a debolted sports route to give *Sexed Up* at E6 6b. Proving that the headpointing ethic might 'keep alive' older traditional routes, Mike Tweedley and Dave Redpath succeeded in a twin 'redpoint' ascent of the classic Dalriada E7 on the Cobbler (see the feature).

Ben Litster repeating Requiem E8, Dumbarton Rock

North West

In Glen Nevis, Dave MacLeod climbed a new E8 in June called *Inimitable*, on the Styx buttress. Ian Taylor found a couple of new routes: *Flotsam* E6 6b left of *Sound of the Surf* in the First Geo at Sheigra and *The Bonus* E5 6a at Reiff, taking the wall right of *Losgaidh* on the Leaning Block. Niall McNair and Iain Small both repeated Ian Taylor's big route *The Eightsome Reel* at Goat Crag. They both fell off quite a few times at the crux (see pic). A split grade of E5/6 was confirmed! In Glencoe, Guy Robertson & Blair Fyffe discovered a three star, four pitch E4 named *Bunjee,* taking a superb cracked wall right of the first stance of *Yo Yo* - destined to become a new classic of the Coe.

Niall McNair on Eightsome Reel E6, Goat Crag > Pic Ian Taylor

North East

In the Cairngorms the Julian Lines classic slab terror of Firestone saw two impressive solos, one from Gaz Marshall and another from in-form Kev Shields, both after pre-practise top-roping. Lochnagar saw Guy Robertson & Adrian Crofton finding routes on a steep wall on the left side of The Stack, overlooking the Left Branch of Black Spout. *Ultramontane* gave a 50m E4 and *Heliopolis* E3 took the obvious groove and superb quartz dyke wall. The Dubh Loch also saw a new addition with Gordon Lennox & Tim Rankin both leading the crux pitch of *Devolution* E6 6b, the fantastic crackline left of *Flodden* on Broad Terrace Wall (Gordon onsighting the crux pitch). On the Aberdeen seacliffs Tim Rankin climbed a new E8 7a called *Steel Armed Android*, taking a 'stunning line up the overhanging prow of Arthur Fowlie between South Crack and Main Crack'. At the same seacliff venue, he also added *Saruman* E4 6a and *The Spell* E3 6a. New routes were *Merlin* E2 by Russ Birkett and *Super Hang On* E5 6b by Rankin. Daniel Laing managed a ground up DWS of *Hole in The Wall* at Longhaven. This E5 (F7a+) saw him in the North Sea four times before he met with success, just before hypothermia set in!

Guy Robertson on Ultramontane E4, Lochnagar > Pic Adrian Crofton

Tim Rankin on Steel Armed Android E8, Pic Neil Morrison

Route Feature: Dalriada E7 6b

An Arrochar mega-route on the Cobbler's distinct blade of terrifying schist, *Dalriada* saw a twin ascent from Mike Tweedley and Dave Redpath on June 1st 2009. Taking advantage of some settled dry summer weather, they headpointed the route over 3 days, Dave noting:

'... we climbed the route headpoint style over three days, the first of which involved an atmospheric session in a gale force wind. On June 1st both tied onto the sharp end to lead it. Tweedley had a minor wobble on the top howling as he nearly pumped off the head wall. Redpath made a hash of the initial arête nearly pumping off and dropping a crucial cam. His composure was regained on the steeper ground to finish the route. Who says headpointing is easy?'

In 1955 this inaccessible prow of rock was worked by Mick Noon and Creagh Dhu members, creating a winding way through the overhang via three hard aid pitches, naming it *The Nook Direct*. It would be a full forty years before a free ascent of the prow direct. 1995 saw a long dry summer spell which culminated in a free ascent of the prow (in redpoint fashion with gear in) by a fit Gary Latter on 20th September.

Dalriada has since seen a number of varying styles of repeat. A second ascent by Dave MacLeod removed the number of pegs from 9 to 2 and placed gear on the lead, pushing the grade closer to E8. Dave noted of this style of ascent:

With the reduced pegs, there is the danger of a 30 foot fall from the base of the headwall onto a small peg. A 40 foot fall onto a short knife blade is possible from the final moves. If both pegs rip, the result would be a 40 metre fatal fall... the climbing is easy for a route at this level but falling off near the top is a big gamble.

Niall McNair bravely attempted an onsight repeat, failing narrowly, managing to climb the route second go ground-up, an impressive achievement. Visiting Lakeland climber Bill Birkett also managed a quick fourth repeat in 2004 - though with full use of pegs a grade of E6 6b had been mooted. Dan McManus attempted a ground-up ascent but fell on the bottom section. The route seems to have 'averaged out' at a consensus grade of E7, but anyone standing underneath this imposing blade of rock will reckon it merits an intimidation point or two! Dave and Mike's 2009 redpoint ascent noted the use of 7 pegs and 7 natural gear, thinking the top-rope 'sport' grade to be about F7b. The first true onsight ascent still remains the biggest challenge in the Southern Highlands...

❑ **Mike Tweedley on Dalriada, Photo Dave Redpath**

Film of the Year
'Single Handed'

The highlight of November is the annual Edinburgh Mountain Film Festival and Scottish film of 2009 was Paul Diffley's documentary on 'disabled' climber Kevin Shields called 'Single-Handed', which features in the DVD 'Monkey See Monkey Do'. Despite being born with most of his left hand missing, Kevin has shocked the climbing world with some daring and inspirational ascents in the last few years. The film exposes Kevin's motivations and follows his progression through the climbing grades, culminating in a gripping and palm-sweating attempt to solo an E6 in Glen Nevis. Also included on the DVD is his remarkable solo of the terrifying Cairngorm slab testpiece 'Firestone' E7.

❏ **Kev Shields soloing The Fatal Kiss E4, Quadrocks**
Photo courtesy Steven Gordon

'Monkey See Monkey Do'
Featuring: 'Single Handed'
Hotaches Procutions 2009

£19.56

Available from:
www.hotaches.com
www.stonecountry.co.uk

People often ask me about how I manage to become bold for climbing and this is going to be different for every bold climber, but I do not see myself as bold. I put myself in risky situations because I feel I owe it to myself for not sticking up for myself early enough as a kid when I was being bullied. So if you look at all the above issues they are countered by the mirror image of themselves: self hate diminished by love of climbing, loneliness quenched by loneliness and self-perceived cowardice confronted by my boldness in soloing close to my absolute physical and mental limits...I also had to try explain to myself how far I'm willing to go to climb a route, the risk, purposeful depression, severing contact with important people in the build up and came very quickly to the conclusion that those fleeting seconds of pure undiluted happiness after the climb are worth all the sacrifice....'

Kev Shields on soloing

❏ **Kev Shields**
Photo courtesy Steven Gordon

Martin Forsyth on Pond Life
Photo Kevin Howett

Craig More West Wall

Craig More, Crieff

Ambience: 'On Golden Pond'
Rock: dolerite
Season: dry spell spring & autumn
Gear: trad rack
Grades: Severe to E2
GetaMap: NN855189

This excellent wee crag lies about 800 metres west of Bennybeg, about 2 miles from Crieff just off the A822. It is part of the same dolerite fault that forms Bennybeg but here the rock has weathered to better, more continuous lines with more natural protection. Pleasant, interesting climbing in a beautifully unspoilt woodland setting overlooking Drummond Pond makes this an excellent low to middle grade crag. All routes by Martin Forsyth and Kev Howett 2006. Routes described right to left.

Access: Park in the dedicated climbers parking area right beside the end of Benny Beg crag (100m north of the Ceramic Experience). From the climber's car park, cross the main road and go over a wall beside large wooden gates. Follow a slight track along the forestry edge to its end, then cut through woods westwards, skirting a wall to the lake. Skirt the right edge of this and as the ground starts to rise the east end of the crag comes into sight.

CONSERVATION NOTES
This area has numerous conservation designations: SSSI (Site of Special Scientific Interest), RAMSAR site and SPA (Special Protection Area). This is primarily for Drummond Pond and its surrounding wetlands and the geese it attracts in winter, but also for epiphytic lichens (those that live on trees) and some rarer rock lichens as well. The established routes climb the clean plant free areas whilst other sections of the crag have a variety of lichens and plants. Do not garden the crag and limit climbing to the established routes. Bolts are unnecessary. Although most of the established routes have solid exits, the crag edge is delicate in places. As most routes follow slight diagonal crack lines it would be best not to bottom rope to ensure both the crag edge and the trees and their lichens at the top are not damaged. If you cannot avoid bottom-roping use slings round trees that reach well over the lip of the crag. Abseiling would cause damage and should be avoided. There is also some nesting bird interest and you are encouraged not to wander too far to the west of the crag during the nesting season in spring and summer. This is not a suitable crag for groups due to site sensitivity and the limited parking shared with Benny Beg.

❑ **1. Painful Memories**   25m VS 4b
The obvious line of weakness on the right edge of the east wall. Start 3m right of *Crocs* to finish just left of the huge oak tree overhanging the wall.

❑ **2. Crocs in the Loch** ❂   25m VS 4c
The blocky crackline of east wall. Gain the crackline, then through the large fault to twin diagonal cracks in the headwall to finish out left at the very top.

❑ **3. Pecker Up**   25m VS 4c
East wall. Up the lower fault right till under the line of a vertical seem parallel to the cracks of Crocs. Up the centre of a smooth wall. Cross the big fault then up the wall to just below a ledge. Traverse hard right into a crack and diagonally rightwards to the 2nd oak tree.

❑ **4. Swan Song**   18m HVS 5a
The right side of the west wall. Up easy rock to a small diagonal crack leading to a horizontal break at half height. Up the wall to a small ledge and a recess. Then upper wall to the right end of a ledge near the top.

❑ **5. Follow the Wild Geese Home** ❂ 18m HVS 4c
The centre of the west wall right of the chimney. Gain the curving crack, step left to a spike under a tiny roof. Thin crack above the roof to a ledge and up to tree. (*Scum on the Edge* 18m E1 5b An eliminate squeezed between *Pond Life* and *Wild Geese* up blankest rock).

❑ **6. Pond Life** ❂   15m VS 4b
The central chimney of west wall. Exit steeply left near the top where the chimney is barred by a roof, into a deep recess to finish. Excellent.

❑ **7. Hung Like a Blue Bell**   15m E2 5b/c
Steep wall left of chimney. Climb right edge of the wall up to small ledge. Up hairline cracks to slot in yellow rock. Left to bigger crack to a small niche, then up left to step into the final thin crack in the headwall.

❑ **8. Idle Vice**   15m E1 5b
The left side of the steep wall. Up direct to the left end of ledge. Left crack up the wall to a final deeper crack.

❑ **9. Earthly Delights** ❂   15m HS 4c
The excellent slight vertical groove line of 'bubbly' rock running into a steep crack, then a ramp to finish.

❑ **10. Drummond Terrace**   15m Severe 4a
The large right trending diagonal shelf near the left end, exiting left at the top under a small tree.

❑ **11. Vixen**   15m VS 4c
Up the large diagonal shelf of *Drummond Terrace* then step left to crack in the slab. Follow this with interest.

Ade Crofton on 'Geriatrics' E2

❑   **1. Sideslip**   20m VS 4b
The left hand line up ramp then up curved crack.

❑   **2. Sideline**   20m VS 4c
From the ramp move direct up the walls left of co⬤

❑   **3. Juggernaut**   25m E1 5a
Wall to ledge, past hole then arête right of corner.

❑   **4. Bloodlust Direct** ☻   30m E2 5b
Climb the groove left of black streaks to a huge
above a ledge, take the leaning red wall above or
pockets to top. Going left from hole is *Juglust* HVS

❑   **5. Maytripper** ☻   30m E1 5b
Step right to zig zag cracks then finish up the
through Bloodlust ramp.

❑   **6. Bloodlust**   30m E1 5a
From the hole of 4, travel right on juggy pocke
ramp and finish diagonally right.

❑   **7. Geriatrics** ☻   40m E2 5b
From belay ledge step left onto wall, up to gear, trav
left along cave lip then up wall right of black strea⬤

❑   **8. Presumption** ☻   40m E2 5b
As for *Geriatrics* but direct up wall to the overlap, fi
up the corner groove and headwall.

❑   **9. Exorcist**   40m E2 5b
As for *Geriatrics* to gear then climb the black str
above through the overlap to higher groove.

❑   **10. Dark Angel**   35m E1 5b
From belay step left round corner to take the
groove to shelf. Final steep corner is the crux.

❑   **11. Black Night**   30m HVS 5a
The big black corner above belay ledge to easy
and final corner on right.

❑   **12. Dolphins & Whales**   30m E4 6a
Steep wall direct. Diagonal pockets to break, gain
pocket left of arête. Crux pockets and slots to top.

❑   **13. Shark Crack** ☻   30m HS 4b
Ab. to ledge 5m above water. Climb the cracked
corner to a steep juggy finish.

❑   **14. Fingers**   30m VS 5a
Ab to slabby ledges. Climb the thin crack up the
right of the corner of *Shark Crack*.

Sheigra 'Second Geo'

□ *Bloodlust Direct E2*

Ambience:	'summer cruising'
Rock:	multi-coloured gneiss
Season:	summer
Gear:	full rack, two 50m ropes, ab rope
Grades:	V Diff to E4. Best grade E2.
GetaMap:	NC 180 604

The furthest north west you can go by road in Scotland ends at a machair campsite by a rocky inlet known as Sheigra. Lewisian Gneiss and Torridonian sandstone swap places every few miles or so along this coastline, but the most attractive rock and crags are the sea-bitten red gneiss walls just north of Sheigra Bay, especially at the gobsmacking 'Second Geo'. This ancient rock is full of pockets and generous solid jugs, so ridiculously steep ground can be climbed in the low extremes. The immaculate rock and the crashing surf makes for atmospheric summer climbing and these classic routes are a must for any aspiring E2 leader, providing wild controlled exposure without the desperation of pumping out in extremis.

Access: from Rhiconich on the A838 an hour and a bit north of Ullapool, take the left turn signed to Kinlochbervie. Follow this single road through Achriesgill and Badcall and once in Kinlochbervie, take a right up past the hotel towards Oldshoremore. Folow the road for a further 5km or so to the road-end. Fresh water and toilet facilities can be found at the Sandwood Bay path parking but camping is perfect down on the machair. To find the second geo, walk north up over the hill by the fences to a rocky plateau. At a giant red boulder on the cliff-top, you will see the crag on the left above a sloping rock platform. Some routes on the far right require a 35m abseil down the corner of Black Night to an obvious black pedestal shelf belay, belaying on the end of the abseil rope. Many routes can be combined or alternative meanderings on jugs is common!

❑ **Pabbay > Banded Geo > Parties on Geomancer E6 (L) & Ship of Fools E5 (R) > Pic Richie Betts**

The Hebrides

The traditional yearly June trip to Pabbay and Mingulay saw a number of strong parties visiting in good weather in 2009 to enjoy some of the best seacliff climbing in Britain, including a strong Sheffield party, complete with T-in-the-Park style party tent and beer kegs. Karin Magog and Steve Crowe climbed a few new E4's and E5's but most parties were content to repeat the now-classic main lines on this paradise of gneiss seacliffs. In 2008 Dun Mingulay saw a repeat of one of the hardest lines in the Hebrides: *Perfect Monsters*, an E7 climbed (1 PA) by Twid Turner, Louise Thomas and Gary Latter in 1998. The second ascent was the first totally free ascent from Carlos Simes & Nils Guillotine. On Barra, over 100 new seacliff routes were found by Colin Moody, Pete Whillance, Karin Magog and Steve Crowe.

Neil Morrison on the False Stack Arch 'Ain't No Strange as Folk', Yesnaby, Orkney

chnagar' by Adrian Crofton

etimes you can be spoilt for choice driving
Deeside. Rattling up towards Ballater with
s crammed in the boot, packs bulging with
s, wire brushes and leaking camelbaks.
have to slow down and decide: Dubh Loch
hard classics? Lochnagar to explore? Or a
ical mystery tour on Beinn a' Bhuird? The
off for the Pass is coming up, spin the wheel
rtune: the sun is shining and the crags are
. Lochnagar it is.

e to Glas Allt, then up by the burn with the
on our backs, the path taking us higher into
lonely crucibles of Lochnagar, and thence
plateau with views clear and far. Strong cool
ds dissuade us from trying the 6b jamming
ks of *Steep Frowning Glories*. We find a fine
n piece of rock tucked away in the lee of
plateau at the top of Black Spout where
Stack forms the right wall of Crumbling
ny. The arête looks like it'll go. We ab from
nvenient thread at the edge of the plateau:
rock looks sound and clean. Guy has first
– swinging into steep cracks from the left
e, precise technical climbing on a steep wall
good protection, the swing back onto the
e, the rock redder, finely edged, bolder but
steep leading up to a sloping ledge and
te, of sorts. A very hard move off undercuts
ain the hanging corner, more good runners
more technical climbing up the groove
ain the belay from which an easier but
osed pitch off left gains the plateau.

down for more – an obvious groove on the
round the corner to the left gains a hanging
e, I undercut this to gain its right edge which
s a cracked ramp line leading to a halfway
k and a good cam. Looking up, the line is
ked by a slim vein of quartz up a blank-
ing wall, I make moves up on thin layaways,
tantly turning back and forth finding the
nce to extend to the next rounded layaway.
I'm far above protection, the climbing
eversible, with the belay ledges still 20 ft
y or more. I give myself a stern talking to,
as I step up I laugh out loud. A 2 ½ friend is
ged into a perfect gas pocket and the rest
smiles...

Routes: Ultramontane E4 & Heliopolis E3

◳ Guy Robertson new routing on the Lochnagar

'...we left our sacks and started off in rubbers for the climb, aiming at the foot of a prominent S-shaped crack...It is a formidable crack, soon approaching the vertical. The final upward move onto the slab on the right was very awkward and exposed. We were now about the centre of the steep lower cliff, in a comfortable and agreeable situation, with a splendid view over the nearer hills across the Firth of Clyde, but with no answer to the urgent question: where next?'

J H B Bell on Cir Mhor's
South Ridge 1945

❑ Angus Murray below the crux roof of West Flank Route, Arran

Arran Cir Mhor Classic Routes

South Ridge Direct ☯
Grade: VS ('Y'Crack short 5a technical crux)
Gear: 50m Ropes, Large Cams, Rocks & Slings
Climb Time: 3-4 hrs
GetaMap: NR 975 431
Notes: This classic safe route has distinctive pitches on perfect granite. Start at the base of the buttress at slabby rock and corners.

1. Easy to a large ledge just right of 'S' Crack. **2.** Enjoyable 'S' crack via deep pocket to ledges. **3.** The 'Y' crack to a fisty fight through roof. **4.** Traverse left on easy slabs to overlap corner. **5.** Memorable 'Layback Crack' and along a juggy vein out right to ledges. **6.** Climb the obvious '3-Tier' blocky chimney above to a crux groove pull onto easy ridge. **7.** Easy scrambling to grassy 'escape terrace'. **8.** Undercut onto a slab up to grass ledge. **9.** Up left to a corner and belay above this. **10.** Slabs right lead to exposed but easy chimney over east face to summit.

West Flank Route ☯
Grade: HVS (technical 5a Pitch 2 & 4)
Gear: 50m Ropes, var. Cams, Rocks & Slings
Climb Time : 2-3 hrs
GetaMap: NR 975 431
Notes: Memorable! Start at the base of big (often wet) flake corners in slabby west face.

1. Up the tricky corner to belay after 15m. Can be avoided by slabs on right if wet. **2.** Puzzling and awkward chimney flake! Contortions lead to good belay ledges. **3.** Long fun diagonal slab crack to belay at niche on right of roof. **4.** Pull over niche left into a cracked groove, layback up right crack, then delicately left over slabs to belay under the big roof. **5.** Traverse left under roof to turn a bulged edge to slabs, belay under high overlap. **6.** Pull through the big overlap and take easy slab crack to the terrace.

Cir Mhor West Flank Climbs

1. South Ridge Direct
2. Anvil Recess Route
3. West Flank Route
4. Souwester Slabs
5. Arctic Way
6. Caliban's Creep

Cult Hero of the Past:
Craig Parnaby

Craig Parnaby blazed onto the climbing scene in the mid 90's. He was inimitable and his ability on rock was terrifying. He started getting strong at the Bowderstone in the early 90's, cruising laps on the classic 6a crack problem for warm-ups. He was a youth from Coniston in the Lakes, with Gecko hands and lithe forearms, reminding you instantly of Ron Fawcett's build - you could just tell he had the genetics.

Even as a beginner he moved on the rock like a bent bow, always tensioned, never loose and arse-out-the-window like the rest of us. He came to Glasgow, ostensibly to study medicine, but he set about dismantling reputations in his own casual and unassuming manner. Over his few years of active climbing he onsighted some of Britain's hardest rock climbs, never once pre-inspecting and rarely seeking beta, he just got on with it. One weekend he went down to Wales and onsighted *The Bells, The Bells*, saying it was 'rather easy', in the manner of a gifted schoolboy rolling his eyes at simplistic homework.

In 1996 he visited Glen Coe. He 'warmed up' by onsighting *Uncertain Emotions*, *Fated Path* and *Admission*, at one point down-climbing a crux because he 'hadn't done it right'. Then it was off to the Freak-Out wall to despatch *Crocodile*, *Jimmy Blacksmith* and *Supernova* before being dragged away to the pub by a knackered second. Craig hated the pub, it was missing good climbing time and he sat there flicking through guide-books 'oohing' at E7's.

Craig ate up the climbing grades like a mumbly-mouthed Pacman eating dots. He began to travel and climb widely, doing big repeats, taking the odd legendary fall, getting back on, doing the E6 or whatever, always persistent, always onsight,

taking his time. His favourite trick was to arrive at climbing wall bouldering comps, climb to the crux, mutter a little, downclimb to the starting jug, shake-out and repeat this until he had solved the problem or the bored queue behind him moved on. He was barred from future boulder comps.

None of us could keep up with Craig's stamina and hunger. He was not afraid to take a fall or two either. One time at Auchinstarry, after a warm-up on *Nijinski*, he fell off the direct start to *Blade Runner*, landing on his head on the plinth below. He rubbed his head a little, inexplicably said sorry to the belayer and despatched the route with one piece of gear in disdain. He continued to motor through the bigger British extremes until his parents took away his ropes and gear and insisted he concentrate on his studies. He dutifully packed away climbing like a worn pair of boots and moved on with his career. But hell, he was a good climber...

Cult Book of the Year:
British Mountaineering
by Claude E. Benson 1909

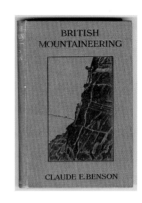

This is a centennial nod to grander times. Published 100 years ago in 2009, Claude Benson's superb 'British Mountaineering' was a richly illustrated climbers' guide to becoming the complete mountaineer. It also included a chapter on bouldering no less, though they did call it 'rock gymnastics', as though they were slightly ashamed of these low-ball games. The book is a delight throughout, capturing the lost nuances of climbing as it was with no little humour and some sage advice. What is most encouraging is that not much has changed - Claude is still obsessed with gear and he bores rigidly about techniques and does witter on a bit in very un-PC terms about the 'tweenie maid'. Reassuringly, however, he seems to suffer the same frustrations we still do today:

"A new rope is troublesome. It kinks most obstinately."

"Gaiters - No one who has worn puttees will ever think of gaiters again. Some people use Fox's Spiral Puttees, but, personally, I prefer the coarse Tommy Atkins' puttee as being better fitted for the rough work, as well as cheaper..."

"I am blest with a basement staircase of stone, and at various points of the day I am to be found hanging by my fingertips to the outside thereof."

"I recommend all who can to imitate me. Let not false shame prevent them. Let them be bold, and brave the suppressed laughter of the tweenie maid."

"Shirts - Flannel is the best material. Those made to take a detachable collar are the neatest."

"Rope - there is only one kind of rope, the very best, the Alpine Club rope. It is to be purchased at Arthur Beale's, 194, Shaftebury Avenue, London, W.C., or at accredited agents."

"Rucksacks - See that there are separate pockets in the rucksack. It is just as well to keep your lunch, your hair brush, and your slippers apart."

"Most of the dangers connected with British mountaineering are unjustly debited to rock-climbing. This is a mistake and a mischievous mistake."

"Never despise the smallest foothold. A 'toe-scrape' may make just the difference of getting up or down..."

"As a matter of fact, provided a man can go steadily and safely, I think he may be entrusted with the care of his own legs and feet without printed regulations, and the same is true of the position of his hands on the axe. Sitting glissades are generally deprecated, though there is no form more common amongst beginners except that on the broad of the back..."

John Watson on the Cluanie Boulder

Bouldering

Scottish Bouldering continues to shake out great blocs from the giant geological Lego box. With classic areas such as Dumbarton continuing to provide cutting edge testpieces, the rest of the country has been explored by visitors and locals alike to reveal the unlimited potential of our wee hilly country. The Hebrides have an untapped potential limited only by their remoteness, whereas the North West coastal glens such as Torridon continue to allow climbers access to immediate new territory. Plenty of remote giant stones have been discovered and await the arrival of intrepid posses of bematted beasts, though the lazy roadside boulderer must find a more adventurous spirit to find the best stones! Glen Nevis is perhaps our best bouldering glen, with many new problems and just as many new stones awaiting development. Dave MacLeod is currently working his way towards a Font 8c in Scotland, likely to be found in this glen. Or will Malc beat him to it at his old haunt of Dumbarton? Aside from our superstars happily crunching away at these abstracted grades, bouldering at any level in Scotland comes with an added bonus: the landscape. The impressive scenery and spirit of place in Scotland still allows the boulderer to enjoy a limitless freedom of movement and a deep sense of harmony. Despite our modern mania for recording everything, there is still a deep well of anonymity and exploration, and many boulder in Scotland for this very reason. This is perhaps its greatest gift.

Scottish Bouldering Scene

In spring 2009, on the Corrie boulders in Arran, Niall McNair found the solution to the Roof boulder's right hand line at 7b+ to give the hardest problem to date on Arran. Having missed his ferry, he aptly named it 'BST'. He also despatched the hanging arete by the fence on the giant *Clach Dhruim a Charn* at 7a+.

Torridon's Ship Boulder > Malc's Arete

In July 2009 Dave MacLeod bagged a rival traverse to his own *Big Long Now* at Sky Pilot (2008) - the ridiculously brutal limestone traverse at Kentallen crag. He described it as: 'classic 8b+/ Font 8a if you are good at undercuts and kneebars. It reminds be of a burlier, and longer (35 metres) version of the classic *Staminaband* at Raven Tor, but with a rather more impressive outlook...' Dave also succeeded on a new 8a+ extended traverse of the Chasm boulder, as well as some new 8a+'s in Glen Nevis.

The South West saw the completed development of the *Rankin Bloc*, the giant granite stone in the Galloway Forest Park on the Queen's Way (see feature). Roddy MacKenzie reclimbed a few of Tim Rankin's earlier problems, then added some of his own trademark testpieces on this fine lump of granite beside the mountain-bike 'black run' track.

The Chasm Boulder Glencoe

On the online side of things there is a new Dumby bouldering site. Jonathan Bean is working on a site to rival Bleau Info, with grade voting, topos, videos etc. It can be found at *www.dumby.info* Remote boulder hunter Lee Robinson is building a huge bouldering database for Britain and Ireland at *www.betaguides. com* which will be going live end of 2009. On it will be downloadable topo booklets for every area imaginable, including many new areas in Scotland (see the Culduie feature).

Beinn Alligin Blocs > Pic www.betaguides.com

Bouldering at Dunkeld saw some attention in 2009 with a terrific line discovered and climbed by Mike Lee to give *Electric Feel* Font 7b+. The problem is located on an attractive scoop of rock 50m downhill in the woods from Cave Crag (turn the corner past the cave howff and meander downhill randomly till you find it!).

In the Trossachs, John Watson visited the Achray Blocs to crank out the superb *Autumn Arête 7a* and various 7b link-ups. At Craigmore he added the direct overlap to *Wide-Eyed* at 7a and repeated the desperate dyno *Surprise Attack* 7b after about a hundred tries!

John Brown continued the Cullen Caves development with a fine 7a with a grotty name *Cullen Skank*! This venue, found on the west flank of the Cullen beach just before Bow Fiddle Rock, has a lot of steep potential.

Akita Boulder > Sheigra > Pic Richie Betts

❏ Mike Lee on Electric Feel at Dunkeld

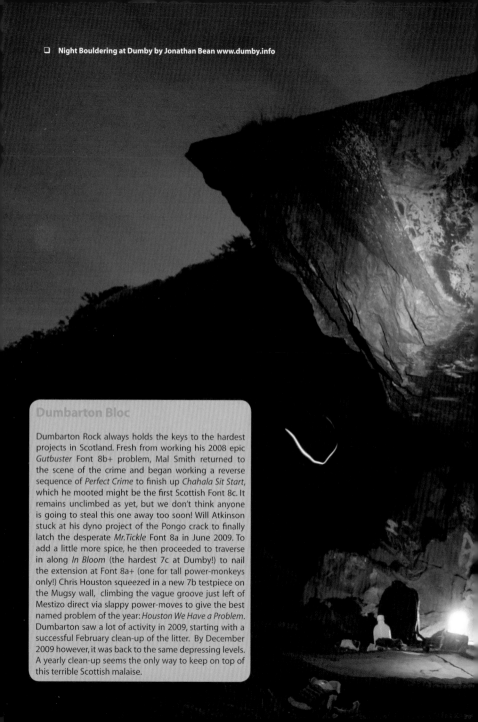

Dumbarton Bloc

Dumbarton Rock always holds the keys to the hardest projects in Scotland. Fresh from working his 2008 epic *Gutbuster* Font 8b+ problem, Mal Smith returned to the scene of the crime and began working a reverse sequence of *Perfect Crime* to finish up *Chahala Sit Start*, which he mooted might be the first Scottish Font 8c. It remains unclimbed as yet, but we don't think anyone is going to steal this one away too soon! Will Atkinson stuck at his dyno project of the Pongo crack to finally latch the desperate *Mr.Tickle* Font 8a in June 2009. To add a little more spice, he then proceeded to traverse in along *In Bloom* (the hardest 7c at Dumby!) to nail the extension at Font 8a+ (one for tall power-monkeys only!) Chris Houston squeezed in a new 7b testpiece on the Mugsy wall, climbing the vague groove just left of Mestizo direct via slappy power-moves to give the best named problem of the year: *Houston We Have a Problem*. Dumbarton saw a lot of activity in 2009, starting with a successful February clean-up of the litter. By December 2009 however, it was back to the same depressing levels. A yearly clean-up seems the only way to keep on top of this terrible Scottish malaise.

Dumbarton's top-end now looks like this:

- ❑ Gutbuster 8b+
- ❑ Supersize Me 8b
- ❑ Sanction 8b
- ❑ Pressure 8b
- ❑ Serum of Sisyphus 8a+
- ❑ Chahala SS 8a+
- ❑ Sabotage 8a+
- ❑ Sosho 8a+
- ❑ Mr. Tickle Ext. 8a+ (8a dyno)
- ❑ Perfect Crime 8a
- ❑ King Kong 8a
- ❑ Pongo Sit Original 8a
- ❑ Hokku 8a
- ❑ Firestarter 8a
- ❑ In Bloom 7c+
- ❑ Silverback 7c
- ❑ Spam 7c
- ❑ Shield SS 7c
- ❑ Consolidated Ext. 7c

Notable 2009 repeats included: *Sabotage 8a+* Will Atkinson, Ben Litster, Stewart Brown, Mark McQuade. *Pongo SS Original 8a* Ben Litster, Chris Houston, Will Atkinson, Mark McQuade. *In Bloom 7c+* Ben Litster, Will Atkinson, Mark McQuade, Andy Shanks. *Spam 7c* Andy Shanks, Stew Brown, Will Atkinson.

Dan Varian on Tears from the Compound Eye

Torridon

Possibly the most exciting bouldering gold rush in Scotland. Hundreds of short crags, roofs, blocs and prows line the endless terraces of Liathach, Seana Mheallan, Beinn Eighe and Beinn Alligin.

Lee Robinson visited the massive boulder cluster under Beinn Alligin. Describing the area as a 'giant amphitheatre of boulders sitting under the jewelled mountain consisting of dense clusters and scattered free standing boulders with good clean rock. Easily found following deer paths below the horns of Alligin. Listen to the underground streams and beware of the frogs!' Park at NG 869 576 next to the river near Torridon house, cross the bridge and take the path north along the river until you reach the base of the ascent to the horns of Beinn Alligin, the boulder field will be in view to the West, head for a large boulder with heather on top in the middle of the main cluster (NR 868 603). The best problem he found was the dynamic 'Utterly Preoposterous' 6b up a tall scooped pillar high in the field, but there are hundreds of projects!

A Fridge Too Far > Torridon

'Beastmaker' Dan Varian visited Torridon in early 2009 and applied his raw power to unclimbed lines above the Celtic Jumble to give some big testpieces such as *Tears from the Compound Eye* 7b+, *Robert the Brute* 7c, *Pallet Knife* 7b+ and *A Fridge Too Far* 7c+ (the steep arête of the cave opposite the Ship Boulder). Dan is reputedly close to finding the area's first 8a and 8b, so locals take note, he is eating up Torridon's hardest lines! Well done to Dan for driving so far north and exhibiting a strong adventurous spirit.

Seana Mheallan saw some bouldering action on the lower terraces across the River Torridon. Dave Kerr developed some good problems around NG 926 557,. Access this area from the passing place next to the stepping stones you cross for Seana Mheallan. Cross the burn and head south west across the bog for the obvious cracked boulder at the foot of the hill.

Robert the Brute > Torridon

Richie Betts repeated the Applecross tester *Changed Days*, a hard 7b sloper problem on the Russell Boulder at Applecross. He tried the notorious Kishorn Boulder scoop project but as yet this remains unclimbed and is the Kishorn area's biggest challenge. Back in Torridon, Richie also reclimbed *Malc's Arête* after holds snapped to suggest it is more like 7b from the sit/crouch start (the broken hold sits nostalgically on his worktop) and 7a+ from standing, which it always was! *Bench Press* 6b had a direct right hand start added to it to give a better 7a version to this mezzanine problem just opposite the Ship boulder.

Applecross Kishorn Stone > Pic Richie Betts

Sutherland & Outer Hebrides

In the far North West, Ian Taylor and Richie Betts started the development at the attractive 'Land of Giants'. These impressive conglomerate blocs lie on a giant wave platform north of Sheigra under Cnoc an Staca. A range of problems have been done from 6b to 7a or so, but higher harder problems are claused with a 'Joe Simpson' crawl-out should you come a cropper! They are accessed from Sheigra by walking north over the hill of Cnoc an Staca and dropping down through the boulder jumble by the sandstone crags to the shore at NC 183613. In the Hebrides, Adi Gill developed a number of new crags and blocs during a summer trip of 2009:

❑ **Land of Giants Lip Traverse > Pic Richie Betts**

South Harris - Aird Mhighe / Liceasto
Loch Stocanais NGR 124928
OS map 14 Tarbert & Loch Seaforth.

Park off the road just past the big white house and the crag can be seen 200m up the hillside. Approx. 100m long and up to 7m high compact gneiss , roofs walls and arêtes. *Big Licks* 6c at the left end of the crag , cross the big roof from left to right via a sit start. Possibly upwards of 60 problems up to the mid 7's for those with time to spend here.

❑ **Land of Giants L > Pic Ian Taylor**

Eriskay - Crag near Roisinis
NGR 805117
OS explorer map no. 452

Park at NGR 799122 walk west on dirt track then over the moor past a couple of fences for approx 1km. Crag is 40m long up to 6m high, slabby to overhanging with flat grassy landings but a bit moist underfoot. Lots of potential up to 7a plus an arm bursting traverse.

Barra - Clach Mhor Nan Glennan
NGR 699048
OS explorer map 452

❑ **Roisinis Crag Bloc > Pic Adi Gill**

Boulder can be seen from the road when driving north at NGR 705041. Park at NGR 698053 and walk south east up the hillside for 500m until you reach the boulder. East side of boulder needs a good clean to yield anything but looks great and overhanging north side has harder projects.

❑   *Traigh Hard* 🌓   6b
Sit start up the wall to the plate jug on the lip then rockover.

❑   *The Vatersay Boys* 🌓   6c
Sit start the arête from the nice pocket and climb it!

❑ **The Vatersay Boys > Pic Adi Gill**

Aberdeen

The schist and granite caves and crags along the whole seaboard of Aberdeen continue to reveal hard new bouldering and superb training traverses. Tim Rankin & Ali Coull managed to repeat *Twilight Princess*, confirming its 8a grade. Tim also reclimbed *Crimp Like a Chimp* on the Portlethen Sports Wall, which he says is now 7b+. He also spent some time on a traverse into his epic prow *Optimus Prime* 7c+ at Cammachmore Bay, which would surely give the NE another 8th grade armblaster. Clashfarquhar remains popular and the *Big Grey* boulder has seen a number of repeats of the classics such as *Clash Arête Sit Start* 7a+. Marcus Bean repeated Tim's *Light Bulb* right arête named *Tink* 7b+. *Georgie Boy* 7c at Portlethen received ascents from Paul Mathers, James Prowse and Marcus Bean. Amanda Lyons stuck in there to grab her first Font 7b with the classic *The Buzz* and with her power there should be plenty more to come.

❏ **Tim Rankin bouldering at Portlethen**
Photo Tim Morozzo

Inverness

Inverness seems to have seen the most of the new bouldering action from a strong crew. Mike Lee has been developing hard lines wherever he wanders: 2009 saw him climb various new testpieces including Scourguie Wood's *Walk the Dog 7b+* and the Ruthven Boulder's long-standing roof project *'QED' 7c*. He also soloed the highball 'Sare' at Pinnacle Crag, Duntelchaig, an impressive and bold rush of blood - a highball Font 7a+ thought to be more like E7 now the pegs (and holds) have gone. This all follows on from some big repeats such as *Susurrus* 7c and a new testpiece at Duntelchaig called *The Settler*, again at a crimpy 7c.

Trev Woods did a couple of new lines on the Ruthven Stane and Richie Betts did a direct into *Barry Manilow* (*Barry Manilower* 7a+). Luke Fairweather repeated *Walk the Dog* (7b+) at Scorguie and *Farr Side Facet* (7b+). He also did the direct into *Knife Wound* at Duntelchaig, the last project on the wall and graded 7b+.

Farr Side Facet is another of Mike's creations on the new 'Jamie' boulder at Farr (NH 680 310). This impressive bloc was revealed once forestry was cleared and now boasts a number of excellent lines on good gneiss. The best lines are *Farr Side Facet* 7b+ SS, *Breathless* 6b, the obvious hanging crack on the west face and *Gluttony 6a+*, the east face direct.

❑ **Mike Lee on FA of QED**

❑ **Rich Betts on Walk the Dog at Scorguie**

❑ **The Jamie Boulder > Farr**

❑ **Mike Lee on Farr Side Facet > Pic Rich Betts**

❑ **Mike Lee on The Settler > Duntelchaig**

Glen Nevis Bouldering

Dave MacLeod is here seen working what was to be his mega traverse *Big Long Now 8b* at Sky Pilot in Glen Nevis. This roofed crag has seen hardcore attention from our best boulderers, including early development by Dave Cuthbertson. In Glen Nevis, Dave MacLeod, resident Lochaber powerhouse, started his year off with an ascent of the last Heather Hat roof project, after a 2008 success on the sloper project at Sky Pilot (Font 8a+). Alan Cassidy was sheltering from a storm when he found a real bouldering gem in a hidden roof above Cavalry Crack buttress, giving a superb 7b+ he called *The Hurricane Shelter*.

❑ **Shelterstone Circuit Bouldering (problem 9)**

Shelterstone Bouldering

Ambience: remote wilderness
Rock: pink granite perfection
Season: summer
Gear: mat and spotter
Grades: easy to 6b
GetaMap: NJ001015

The route to the Shelterstone is complex and requires good map-reading and high mountain walking skills, especially if you are carrying a mat! The winds can be very strong and dangerous on the Cairngorm plateau, so choose a quiet weather period in summer for exploring these boulders. Access is not recommended in poor weather.

Walk-in 2-3 hours. From the Aviemore ski-centre car-park, the good path trending right (west) up to the neighbouring Coire an t' Sneachda. The path rises into the corrie and eventually through scree and up right under the crags via the steep 'goat-track' up onto the plateau. This is a good hour fast walk at least to get here. Cross the plateau due south (compass vital in mist) down the gradually steepening Coire Domhain, past Hell's Lum crags on the right. Follow the tumbling stream downhill into the Loch Avon basin, where the boulders lie under the mighty Shelterstone crag.

The 'Knoll' area is obvious with grassy and gravel landings close to the shores of the loch - the higher boulders suffer from bad landings. It is a great place for an evening after a day's cragging before retiring to the beach! Harder problems exist but development is slow due to the remote nature of the boulders.

Mobiles do not work in the area, so be sensible about risk-taking - it's a long crawl out should you sprain an ankle or worse. Ideally travel in with a friend for spotting. The Shelterstone itself is a giant boulder in the middle of the scree with a superb howff underneath it, though the bouldering on the bloc is limited itself due mainly to bad landings and cluster. The odd roof may provide a harder problem or two but as of yet no one has reported problems over 7a.

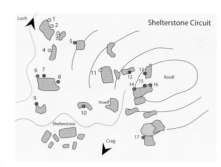

Easy Circuit

- ☐ 1. Easy arête.
- ☐ 2. Overhanging groove, move left.
- ☐ 3. Short slab direct.
- ☐ 4. Bigger slab to the right direct.
- ☐ 5. Cube-shape boulder arête.
- ☐ 6. RH arête of the diagonal crack.
- ☐ 7. R-L traverse and up centre.
- ☐ 8. Overhanging groove.
- ☐ 9. Sharp arête.
- ☐ 10. L-R lip traverse.
- ☐ 11. Easy slab L-R above howff.
- ☐ 12. Short wall on pink crimps.
- ☐ 13. Lip traverse R-L.
- ☐ 14. Traverse crack from R-L.
- ☐ 15. RH side of the Nose.
- ☐ 16. LH side of the Nose.
- ☐ 17. Crack and arête.

Trossachs Achray & Ben A'an Blocs

Ambience:	autumnal lost world
Rock:	quartzy compact schist
Season:	dry, cool day any season
Gear:	one mat, brushes, skin cream
Grades:	accessible testpieces to 7b
OS GetaMap:	Achray Blocs NN504065
	Ben A'an Bloc NN500080

❏ Hocus Pocus 7a at Ben A'an

From Aberfoyle cross the Duke's Pass on the A821 to drop down to the shores of Loch Achray. As the road turns right over a bridge at the Loch Achray hotel, there is an obvious domed crag on the left. The blocs lie hidden on the left of the crag under a large beech tree. There is a small parking spot on the right beside a lakeshore gate, or further along the road at the Ben Venue car-park.

❏   **Spring Board**   4+
Low Bloc. SS the left cave arête and gain jugs on shelf then layback up short arête.

❏   **Autumn Watch**   6c+
Eliminate without arête. SS under left of cave, RH on poor crimp, LH on cave crimp rail. Crux pull on and slap up through crimps to juggy ledge.

❏   **Bill Oddie** ♥   7b
As for *Autumn Watch*, but from crimps snap right to the central lip crimp of *Spring Watch*, use intermediate LH slopey pinch to get into *Spring Watch* finish. A deep SS will be about 8a.

❏ Necker Cube Achray Blocs

❏   **Spring Watch**   6c
Eliminate. Hang the central crimps and boost up and left for a sloping hold just right of the juggy rail (out). Finish up and right via holds on *Autumn Arête*. SS project.

❏   **Autumn Arête** ♥   7a
Right arête. SS at undercut and LH cave crimps. Slap up slopers and crimps to crux crossover sequence on arête tojugs at top.

❏   **Necker Cube**   6a
SS the right wall at good holds, bum on little boulder. Slap up and left to the arête and technically step up on sloper to snatch for top jugs.

❏   **Hocus Pocus** ♥   7a
A further 30 minutes walk up the Ben A'an path to the clearing and downhill under the crags. Climb the attractive lip of the boulder from a ledge SS to a lip traverse to hard rockover onto slab.

❏ Bill Oddie on the Achray Blocs

The Rankin Bloc - Galloway

Ambience: lonesome gem
Rock: ultrabasic granite
Season: spring & autumn
Gear: mat and boots for approach
Grades: easy to 7b
GetaMap: NX 486 710

This excellent giant bloc was discovered by Tim Rankin a number of years ago and sits in amongst the mountain bike trails in the Galloway Forest Park southwest of Craigdews Hill.

Park on the A712 between New Galloway and Newton Stewart at the carpark marked *Talnotry*. This is car park immediately after the *Grey Mare's Tail* car park when heading West, which itself is immediately after the Wild Goat Park. Cross the road and head down the forestry road situated about 50 metres to the East of this car park and walk along this road. After about 5 minutes you'll cross the river and pass the Mountain Bikers' slab.

All problems are shown as starting from the marked holds:

❑ 1. **Boulderdash** — Font 6a SS

❑ 2. **Cowboy Country** — Font 6b

❑ 3. **Crouching Kitten** — Font 6b

❑ 4. **Retroclaim** 🌀 — Font 7a+

❑ 5. **Project** — (Font 7c/8a)

❑ 6. **Project** — (V Hard)

❑ 7. **Bohemian Rhapsody** 🌀 — Font 7b SS

❑ 8. **Broke Back Mountin** — Font 6c (SS 7a)

❑ 9. **Carpet Samples** 🌀 — Font 6b SS

About 1 minute further on from this point you'll reach a small layby on the right of the road. At this point if you look back and down to your right (towards the river) the Rankin Block should come into view. Despite the fact that it is only about 200 metres away from the road you should take your time crossing the ground to reach the boulder. It appears mostly flat and green, but is made up of old fallen trees and moss and as such you may find yourself falling through the surface. Do not wear sandals!!!!

Notes and Development - Roddy MacKenzie 2009

CULDUIE BOULDERING

The Sphinx

betaguides

Nic Ward on Snoddy

Egypt Himself

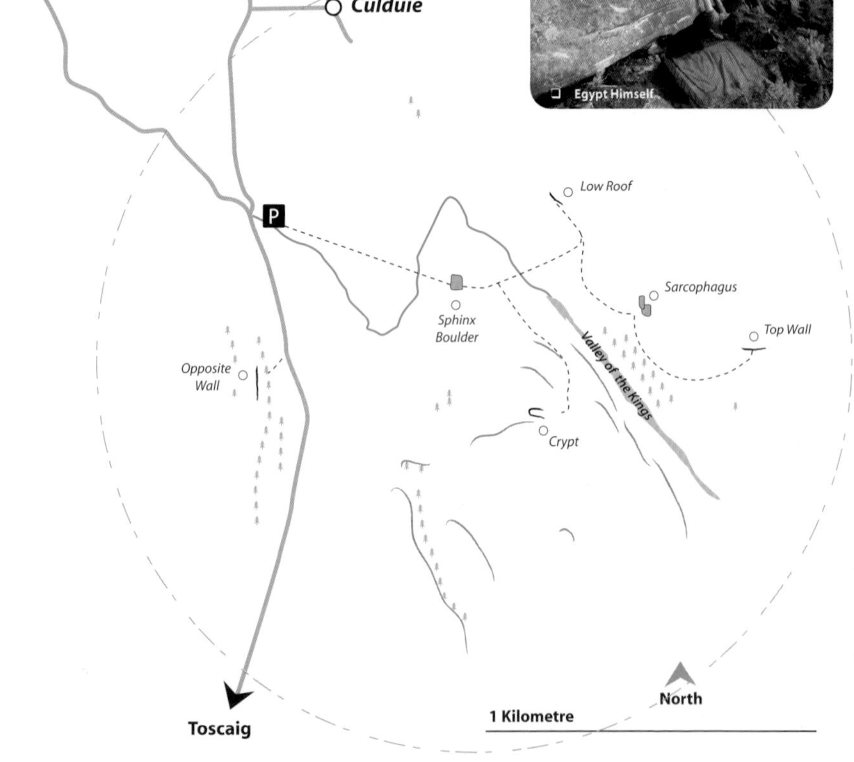

Applecross

Ard-dhubh

Culduie

P

Low Roof

Sarcophagus

Sphinx
Boulder

Top Wall

Opposite
Wall

Valley of the Kings

Crypt

Toscaig

North

1 Kilometre

Culduie Bouldering (Slochd na Beinne)

The Culduie area on the Applecross Peninsula is scattered with small terraces and free standing blocks. The rock is a superb fine-grained Torridonian Sandstone which is easy on the skin. Just south of Culduie there is a fissure, called Slochd na Beinn, named by one of the locals as the *Valley-of-the-Kings*. Problems developed by Nick Ward and Lee Robinson. For more details on Applecross bouldering see **www.betaguides.com**

Approach: Culduie is 3 miles south of Applecross village along the shore road. Drive through Culdie and carry on for another half mile to park just before a bridge. Walk SE towards the entrance of the valley, and the Sphinx boulder will come into view - it is a perfect free standing bloc 100m before the valley. The majority of the bouldering is on the left hand side of the valley. From the Sphinx, cross the wall, then head up the left flank to arrive on the terrace above the large crag.

❑ **The Sphinx** ✆ 6a
Sphinx SE Arête. SS with a large undercut and right-hand sidepull. Pull up left for a good jug, nice top out.

❑ **Lichen Lovers** 6b
Sphinx. SS the NE arête, taken on its right hand side.

❑ **The Crypt** Easy
A walled off sheep-pen type area with perfect 6m high walls - good fun!

The Low Roof GR 722 399
From the top of the steep part of the walk-in to reach the first terrace, continue straight on. Ahead/slightly right you'll see a large broken roof. Head towards it a short way then trend leftwards, cross a burn and ascend the small knoll. You will notice an inconspicuous buttress, but on closer inspection, there is a perfect chest-high roof along its length.

❑ **Sam the Piper** 6c
Low Roof. SS on a low jug, RH to a diagonal hold on lip, and some stiff crimp pulling to finish up the easy top wall.

❑ **Snoddy Caught a Prawn** 7a
Low Roof. SS. Similar to the previous problem, but harder. 1.5m left, pull out of the roof to a small right-hand hold. Stiff pulls up and left lead to an easy finish.

❑ **Ally Brown's Store** 6a
Low Roof. SS. Another 2m left, start at the large holds under the roof. Pull round and up large blocky holds.

Top Wall GR 726 395

❑ **Sloper Project**
At the left hand end is an obvious large sloping ledge. Use sidepulls to gain the height to eventually get established on the ledge. Been done with jugs on the right arête but would be a great tick to stay central.

❑ **Flakes** 3c
Where the wall gets higher there is an obvious set of flake lines trending up and right. Climb them gently.

❑ **Flakes 2** 3c
Just right of the flakes, climb up good holds to make a big move for a ledge and top out.

❑ **Pinnacle** 4a
Next buttress to the right. Sit start just right of the arête, climb up avoiding the arête.

❑ **Thin Wall** 6a
Top walls right. SS. Make a tricky pull to a loose jug and hold above to get established. From small sidepulls make a big move for a good sloping hold high up.

The Sarcophagus Jumble GR 724 396
This area is the jumble of boulders in front of the last large crag which is passed on the approach to the Top Wall. It is situated above a crag which is most easily passed on its right, close to the valley. The most obvious feature is the Sarcophagus boulder which is perched up at 2 sides, creating a through-feature.

❑ **Egypt Himself** 7a+
When approaching the Sarcophagus, a sloping lip feature is clearly visible on the left. SS, right to left traverse on immaculate rock, starting at the low large dish. Grapple your way along by using a combination of grovelling beached-whale tactics hanging from the lip to finally reach the left arête. Pull over. Pull a face.

❑ **Nic's Follow-Through** ✆ 7a+
The through feature of the Sarcophagus boulder. Under the roof is a large flake. Begin as close to the downhill opening of the underside of the boulder as possible. Climb towards the uphill side via jugs and a large move for a right hand sidepull, pull round and top out. For the tick, avoid the arête and sidewall. A brilliant exercise in barbaric thuggery.

❑ **It Takes Tomb to Tango** 6a
The steep low wall right of the previous problem. SS down in the niche, crimp for left and small pocket for right, fire for the enormous jug in the break, then finish using good holds set back from the lip.

CRAIGMORE BLOC

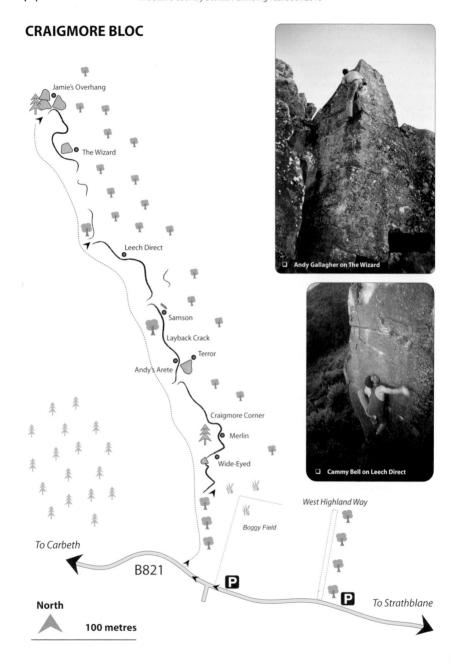

Jamie's Overhang

The Wizard

Leech Direct

Samson

Layback Crack

Terror

Andy's Arete

Craigmore Corner

Merlin

Wide-Eyed

❑ **Andy Gallagher on The Wizard**

❑ **Cammy Bell on Leech Direct**

West Highland Way

Boggy Field

To Carbeth

B821

P

P

To Strathblane

North

100 metres

Craigmore Bloc Glasgow

Ambience: craggy rock heads
Rock: dimpled basalt slopers & crimps
Season: long dry spell
Gear: mats, brushes, mushroom basket
Grades: easy to 7b
GetaMap: NS528798

Approach: From Glasgow take the A809 out of Glasgow through Bearsden into open country to the Carbeth Inn. 200m after this take a right turn onto the B821 link road to Strathblane. Drive past the hut community for 1km and past two bends to open fields (loch on right). Park carefully by the field wall. The crag is north of the road in a small wood under a tree-lined ridge. Walk back up the road (watch out for bikers) and hop a hidden stile to a vague path up under the trees to drop down to the crag.

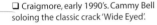

❏ Craigmore, early 1990's. Cammy Bell soloing the classic crack 'Wide Eyed'.

❏ **Wide-Eyed** 6c+
Crinkle-cut crack in the wall. Lunge to the break in the centre and lock-off up to a stretch for reluctant juggy holds, compose and solo or downclimb right. Crack to right is *Harmless* 6a.

❏ **Merlin** 6b+
Round the corner is a blunt arête right of a holly corner. Climb the vertical face on the left of this from small foot ledges, slap up and right to poor hold in the corner, then climb the face and snatch right to jugs.

❏ **Jolly Green Dragon** 6b+
Corners buttress. This excellent eliminate problem sit-starts at a V-hold down right at prop bloc, booms up to tiny finger-sloper in the break, then a crux lunge all the way up to a sloping ledge. Downclimb right.

❏ **Terror** 5+
'Face' bloc by main crag. Gain good incut slots on the arête and reach right, step up on smears and gain the good 'eye' hold on the face, then mantle over on the right or left.

❏ **Terror Right Hand** 7a
More direct and even better. SS the arête with pinch and gain the good slot on the right 'chin', climb the mossy face direct with long reaches and a rockover.

❏ **Andy's Arête** 6c+
The crag arête opposite *Terror* is a real tricky number! SS with pinch and sidepull leading to a tenuous move right to the letterbox jump-off jugs. Sitting start further right at poor sidepulls direct to letterbox is 7a.

❏ **Samson** 6c
Past main crag is a blank wall above an embedded stone. Pull on with poor undercuts and wobble powerfully left to reach and match a V groove. Jump off from jugs.

❏ **Leech Direct** 6b
As crag rises look for a horizontally cracked wall over a ramped corner. Climb to the break, employing faith in hands and feet, or you are trampolined off into the ferns.

❏ **The Wizard** 7a+
Gandalf's hat! SS in the wee cave and use the short right arête to lunge up and right for a poor finger sloper, then join the highball arête finish. Eliminating the cave arêtes makes it a barndoory 7b. Stand start is 6c.

❏ **Jamie's Overhang** (aka *Art of War*) 6c
Bloc under Scots Pine at very end of crag. From the cave's crimpy break snatch almost footless for the good LH hold, heel-hook left and slap up right to the sloper right of apex, sharp RH crimp on slab to rockover.

❏ **Surprise Attack** 7b
SS the central crimps and dyno direct to the sloping lip just right of the apex (no fat sloper on right) and rockover. Cold conditions and patience required to reach the sloper and then hang it.

❏ **The Sun Tzu Dyno** 6c
Jamie's Overhang right hand version is superb. From the break crimps dyno up and right to the fat sloper and rockover via sharp crimp.

Glen Lednock Blocs

Ambience: 'family day oot'
Rock: compact schist
Season: summer or any fine dry day
Gear: mats, wire brushes, skin cream
Grades: good easy blocs for kids, testpieces 6a to 7b
GetaMap: NN727286

Approach: From the A9 Perth-Stirling road, take the exit signed to Braco along the A822. Just after Braco, take a left onto the B827 signed to Comrie. Once in Comrie turn left at a T-Junction after the river. Drive round a sharp bend and at the next bend turn right uphill into the forest. Continue into Glen Lednock proper. Drive 2km to the Invergeldie farm gates and head uphill past the Sput Rolla waterfall. Close all gates behind you and park just before the dam at a U-bend. The blocs lie in clusters on grassy alps across the wee wooden bridge under the dam on the flanks of Creag nan Eun. 5 minutes walk at most. Full topo available from *www.stonecountry.co.uk*

❏   **Tsunami**   7b
The slabby low bloc on the first little plateau amongst the 'Kids' Blocks'. SS at the obvious layaway at wee cave and use slopers up left to get onto the slab. Looks easy, doesn't it? Tim Carruthers 2003.

❏   **Feathering the Penthouse**   6a+
Twin blocs above rocky path: 'The Eiffel Blocs'. This climbs the super hanging thin vertical crack above the track. SS on jams in the deep crack. Up into the thin crack and pull up and right to the top. Kev Howett 2003.

❏   **Best in Toon**   6b+
The flat-faced boulder right of the Eiffel blocs: 'The Lamp Bloc'. SS on the flat hold in centre left, up and right passing a good hold and then into the vertical crack which may need a good brush. Kev Howett 2003.

❏   **Red 22**   6a
Reiver's Bloc is the fine stone on the left of the path overlooking glen. SS glen face at obvious ledge. Gain layaways right of the diagonal crack, LH crimp then go again for a poor LH sloper, heel hook to the apex, pull over.

❏   **Sneak By Night**   6a+
Reiver's Bloc. The slabby right arête itself. Start on a good flat hold at head height in the steeper side wall to the right. Direct up the right side of the arête on small holds, take the edge of the slab to the top.

❏   **Reiver's Logic** ☁   7a+
Reiver's Bloc. SS from the obvious shelf at the base of the arête up to a good RH crimp. Reach diagonally right via hard crimping to a good hold in the centre of the wall, back left to the arête.

❏   **Breaking Wave** ☁   7a
Dam Blocs. A superb problem direct through the centre of the 'wave' feature wall. SS in the centre of the diagonal crack and pull direct through the wave, reach right onto the glacis above on dimples. Kev Howett 2003

❏   **Manic Stupor** ☁   7b
Dam Blocs overhang. Crouching start at two holds in the big curving shelf which runs through the roof. Gain undercut with a sneaky heel-toe & power upwards to the lip, traverse left to rockover. Tim Palmer 2003.

❏   **Keep it Unreal**   7a+
The Real Estate Blocs, lowest bloc in glen. West wall. This hard problem takes the blunt reddish arête SS then layback up the right hand side. Sloping holds. Tim Carruthers 2003.

❏   **Delicatessence**   6a+
Upright bloc is low left in the glen. The main slab via two horizontal cracks. SS on a thin flake and gain the first break, then climb delicately to the second. Reach for jugs at top. Font 5 from standing left. Kev Howett 2003.

⬚ Glen Lednock > Richie Betts on Red 22

Creag nan Eun Blocs

EUN SPUR

Saffire
Kist
Horns of Eun
Reiver Stone
Wee Mans
Curbstone

Real Estate
DRY SLOPE
Split Rock
Upright
Lamp
Squat
Taper
Eiffel
Wave
SLEEPY HOLLOW
BOG
BOG
Flying Bomb

Pyramid
Tsunami

DRY RIDGE

P

Image © Kev Howett

Richie Betts in full dyno at Glen Lednock

❑ **Mal Smith powering his way through Gutbuster Font 8b+, Dumbarton**

This yearbook is the result of many climbers' passion
and dedication. Thanks to:

Guy Robertson www.equipuk.com
Tim Rankin www.transition-extreme.com
Lee Robinson www.betaguides.com
Dave MacLeod www.davemacleod.com
Adrian Crofton www.nemt.org.uk
Dave Redpath www.scottishclimbs.com
Neil Shepherd www.freewebs.com/arbroathclimbing
Neil Morrison www.nemt.org.uk
Paul Diffley www.hotaches.com
Steve Gordon www.stevengordon.eu
Kev Howett www.mcofs.org.uk
Colin Lambton www.creaghdhu.org
Blair Fyffe www.smc.org.uk
Jonathan Bean www.dumby.info
Colin Moody www.colin-moody.com
Tim Morozzo www.morozzo.co.uk
Richie Betts
Pete Benson
Stewart Brown
Ben Litster
Cameron Bell
Roddy MacKenzie
Ian Taylor
Michael Lee
Kevin Shields
Adrian Gill

❑ Stone pavement on Ben More Coigach